Sunset
patio book

Sunset
patio
book
REVISED EDITION

By the editorial staffs of
Sunset Books & Sunset Magazine

LANE BOOK COMPANY
Menlo Park, California

Library of Congress Catalog Card Number: 52-7391

Title Number: 140

Second Edition March 1961

Copyright 1961, 1952

First Printing March 1961

LANE BOOK COMPANY, MENLO PARK, CALIFORNIA

By the publishers of *Sunset* Books and *Sunset*, The Magazine of Western Living

LITHOGRAPHED IN U. S. A.

Contents

Planning

Structure

Planting

Extending

Cover photograph by Clyde Childress (see page 36)

Title page photograph by Maynard L. Parker • Title page patio design by Cliff May

IS IT A TERRACE? A patio may be located next to the house, expanding its livability and drawing into it the light, color, and freshness of the garden.

IS IT AN OPEN AREA? In benign climates a patio may be an opening in the garden, floored with lawn or paving, walled with trees, roofed with sky.

IS IT A SHELTER? A patio may be an enclosed room, open on the side to all outdoors, roofed to exclude weather, provide pleasant living all year.

Just What is a "Patio"?

Ask half a dozen neighbors to define a "patio", and you will probably get a half dozen different answers.

One or two might agree with the dictionary that it is an enclosed court, walled-in by the house, and open to the sky. Someone else will tell you it is a roofless play room located next to the house; and another will contend it is a room of the house itself, with an outer wall missing. Another neighbor may insist that it is a separate structure altogether, placed by itself in the garden, and filled with barbecue gear. Your sixth friend (who probably just moved in from some remote part of the country) may not know what you are talking about. A patio? Never heard of it.

Strangely enough, all of these assorted notions make sense. A patio may be a fully enclosed courtyard, as the dictionary says it is supposed to be. It can be a terrace alongside a house, or a separate garden shelter, or a recreation room of the house itself. Or it can be a loggia or a clearing in the forest. Even the innocent newcomer is entitled to his ignorance: for in many regions, the patio exists under a local name.

Let's pin it down. A patio is first of all an *outdoor* room. It may be set right out in the open, with shrubs and trees for walls, lawn for carpeting, the sky for its ceiling; or it may be roofed over for sun protection, but with its walls left wide open to draw in the freshness of all outdoors.

But a patio is more than a room—it is a pleasant way of life. The very popularity of the Spanish word testifies to the general understanding of its overtones. To many people, the word suggests leisure and lazy-day pursuits. The early patios that the Spaniards built under a benign Western sky were take-it-easy rooms, combination living-dining-barbecue rooms where you relaxed with your friends, sheltered from the summer sun. This is the true heritage of the patio, and even when combined with the mid-western porch, the Yankee summer house, or the Colonial breezeway this amiable flavor persists.

It is in this broad sense that we have used the term in this book. Into it we have rolled terrace, lanai, garden shelter, sun porch, deck, recreation area, barbecue shelter, and all the other close relatives.

This book stresses "how-to-plan-it" rather than "how-to-do-it." Its primary purpose is to present an extensive and diversified collection of ideas that will help the home planner and the home remodeler to decide which type of outdoor room will best suit his needs.

In the photographs that follow, you will see how a couple of hundred families have worked the patio into their daily living. Many of these patios were planned by the homeowners themselves, many are the creations of outstanding architects and landscape architects. Nearly all of them were selected from articles on patios that have appeared in *Sunset Magazine*.

Elements of the Successful Patio

What makes the difference between a passable patio and a successful one that charms you with its pleasant atmosphere? No one thing separates good patios from bad—several factors combine to make the difference. For instance, a *successful* patio is ...

1 Oriented to the Sun

A patio that is oriented to invite or to evade the sun, according to local climate, can be usable throughout much of the year. Screening to block the late afternoon rays benefits any patio.

2 Not Too Big: Not Too Small

There should be room for bulky furniture, for games, for parties, for garden vehicles. Patios need to be scaled to all outdoors.

3 Related to the House

A patio brings light, color, air, and a spacious feeling into the house; draws out of it facilities for cooking, dining, lounging.

4 Fitted Into the Garden Plan

As only one part of the house-garden plan, the patio should be related to service area, work center, play yard, lawns, plantings.

5 Comfortably Furnished

Comfortable and casual furniture add to the take-it-easy atmosphere, contrast with more formal furnishings inside the house.

6 Fenced for Privacy

Screen fencing of wood or growing vine give seclusion and the privacy needed where family living extends to the lot boundaries.

7 Provided with Weather Modifiers

Overhead screens give choice of sun or shade, break up winds. In hot areas, patios need cooling devices; in cold zones, heating.

8 Equipped for Barbecuing

A barbecue adds a focal point to patio living, provides a center for casual dining, for deft showmanship, for memorable cooking.

9 Designed for Children's Play

Patios belong to children, too; and the foresighted designer plans for various ages: sand boxes, then ping pong, later the dance floor.

10 Pleasantly Planted

Trees, shrubs, and plantings make a patio livable with their dappled shade, softening textures, color accents, and fragrance.

11 Provided with an Open Fire

An outdoor fireplace helps to extend the patio hours into the cool evening, brings the fellowship of the camp fire into the home.

12 Paved with Durable Surfacing

Patio paving should be pleasant to look at and walk on; should be non-skid, non-glare, and easy to clean; should dry quickly.

Orientation to the Sun

The enjoyment that you get from an outdoor living room is in direct ratio to your success in controlling the weather.

To control and modify climate, you must work with many factors, but none so important as the sun. The sun must be invited and avoided. You invite its heat in winter; avoid it in summer.

Naturally, the amount of control will differ in various localities. In the even mild climates along the coast, no extensive sun protection on a permanent basis is necessary. Generally, wind control is more important than sun protection. Temporary and portable controls—umbrellas, screens, canvas—add to the usability of outdoor areas.

In the Southwest and in the summer-hot valleys of Central California, the problem is generally too much sun. A southern exposure needs thorough protection from summer sun. Shade also must be given to outdoor areas not only for its own use but to prevent reflected heat.

In some parts of the Northwest, sun is welcome during some of the summer months when misty rains roll in.

Depending on which of these zones you live in, you will basically have need for either a warm or a cool patio. Your choice of site, or modification of an existing one, will determine which of these you will be able to develop.

Orientation of the patio area to the sun is the chief determinant of the weather to be enjoyed there.

Warm South Patio

The sun never deserts a south-facing patio. All day, from sun-up to sun-down, it pours warmth on the outdoor room, regardless of season or latitude.

In mild or chilly climates, this is a boon to outdoor living; but in regions with parching summer weather, the ever-present sun has to be excluded if the patio is to be usable.

Standard means of sheltering the terrace from the sun is an overhead roof of some type. This will exclude direct sun throughout most of a summer day, but it will not bar it in early morning or late afternoon. The slanting rays of the western sun can be blocked with vertical screens, louver panels, or, of course, a wing of the house.

A south-oriented patio needs sun protection during the summer, both from the direct rays overhead and the slanting shafts of late afternoon. This covered patio in Arizona invites the southern horizon into its open wall, but excludes the western sun with a glass-studded wall. The porch-like terrace is 20 feet deep.

Design: Japstad & Knipe
Photo: Frank L. Gaynor

Western exposure is desirable in localities with cool climates. This west-facing terrace, for instance, can be used in winter, for it is a sun-trap, sheltered from prevailing winds—an ideal spot for growing potted plants. A sunscreen of old apple trees overcomes the usual defect of western orientation, the heat and glare of afternoon sun.

Design: Pietro Belluschi
Photo: Ron Partridge

During winter, the low sun finds its way under the overhead and warms the patio sufficiently for many days' use. If an extra heat source is provided, such as an outdoor fireplace, radiant heat panel, or even a charcoal brazier, the number of comfortable patio days can be greatly increased. A southern patio dries out quickly after rains.

If you live in a scorching climate and have only a southern location to develop, you will need to add various cooling devices, such as a drip wall, mist sprinklers, or a vine-laden fence that can be kept moist and serve as a giant desert cooler, when the hot wind blows through it.

Hot Western Patio

A west-oriented patio is likely to be a scorcher in the afternoons, when it receives the full force of the sun's rays.

Up to lunch time, it is a pleasant morning haven; but once the sun passes over the roof top, the patio becomes uncomfortably hot unless provided with a sheltering canopy. Without overhead protection, the sun will slam against the west wall of the house which receives six times as much heat in summer as it does in winter, and radiate into the patio. A vertical sun screen is also needed to block the late afternoon sun, which will pass under an overhead from 3 o'clock on and shine into the house. In a hot climate, it needs all the cooling devices available: evaporating water, reflecting panels, shrubbery.

Western patios are not so successful for winter use as southern ones. The absence of morning sun keeps the west side damp through the rainy months, and prevents its warming up quickly. Good surface drainage, a fireplace, and an adjustable overhead that can be removed to bring in whatever sun is available, will help to make it usable in winter.

Cool Eastern Patio

When the patio faces east it benefits from morning sun and begins to cool off in the afternoon. It is a desirable orientation for a hot climate, for with only a few weather modifiers, it can be made a very pleasant summer retreat. Overhead protection is not essential, unless it is desired as a shelter from rain, fog, or as a means for holding the heat of the day into evening.

Although an east patio will draw the winter sun until well past the noon hour, it may never quite dry out or warm up for free-and-easy winter use.

Southeast-facing outdoor living area is flooded with sun in the morning, but shade begins to take over as the day progresses. For benefit of afternoon sun-seekers, prow-shaped deck was added to original small concrete patio. Those who prefer shade in the afternoon can keep cool under the wide roof overhang.

Design: Eckbo, Dean and Williams
Photo: Phil Palmer

During the summer, a north-oriented patio will draw morning and late afternoon sun. This bedroom terrace is warmed by the early sun, filtered through the oaks and firs. A fresh and sunny spot for a breakfast of pancakes, cooked on the portable grill. Note that bedroom windows face north, escape the alarm-clock rays of the sunrise.

Design: Richard Sundeleaf
Photo: Carroll C. Calkins

If your exposure is eastward and your climate cool, you may need supplementary heating, even in summertime. A fireplace, radiant panel, or possibly some reflecting panels should help.

Cold Northern Patio

Coolest site for a patio is a northern exposure. Part of a north-facing patio never receives any direct sun, even in summer when the sun is on its northward leg. If the patio is in back of a two-story house, the entire patio may pass through the seasons in complete shade.

Because of its sheltered position, it does not need an overhead, except as protection from rain or as a visual necessity. A glass or plastic roof which will shed rain and let in the light, makes an excellent solution.

Some form of heating is almost essential for real enjoyment of this patio. In fact, means should also be provided for conserving the extra heat, such as wing walls that reflect the heat into the patio, or doors that slide across the open side when the weather gets rough.

North patios are essentially hot weather friends, but if they are enclosed, they can extend their usefulness through the entire calendar.

Compromises

These sketches tell only part of the story. Not everyone owns a plot of ground that runs true to the four points of the compass; in some situations, wind is more of a scourge than sun; perhaps there is a view to be preserved, and a decision gives it to the living room windows and forces the patio to take a second-choice location. However, the general characteristics of the four patios discussed above can be used as a rough guide in working out particular situations.

For instance, if you have a north patio in a region of cool climate, why not stretch the floor area into the sun and make a two-ended patio? The new part is a south patio. Or, if you are suffering with a western exposure, swing the patio around the corner and create a new wing on the north side as a retreat from a merciless sun. In the same manner, a south patio can be elbowed around a corner to join with an east patio. For that matter you can also have two independent patios: a warm one and a cool one on opposite sides of the house.

To reduce the glare of high summer sun on this north-facing patio —without cutting down on daylight inside the house—owners erected framework for sliding panels of plastic-coated screening. They can easily be shifted for a varied pattern of sun and filtered sun, and removed in winter.
Photo: Robert Cox

How Large Should It Be?

One of the commonest mistakes an amateur makes in planning his patio is to design one that is too small for his needs. In many situations, of course, the space available on the lot prohibits large-scale development. But when there is plenty of room, the untrained designer often makes too timid use of it.

The amateur is likely to think of the patio in the same terms as an indoor room and to apply the same yardstick to outdoor living as indoor. Usually, this is a mistake—and for several reasons.

To begin with, there is a difference in scale between outdoor and indoor space. Inside the house, you relate your furniture to the walls, floor area, windows, and ceiling; but outdoors, these limits may not exist. Your walls may be 100-foot trees, your ceiling the sky, the floor a 100-square-foot lawn area. This is one reason why groupings of furniture that seem right in the living room may seem dwarfed and spindly in the patio.

A second point that is often overlooked is the fact that outdoor furniture takes up more space, piece for piece, than indoor furniture. Wooden patio chairs, benches, tables, and lounges are bulkier or just plain larger than their indoor counterparts. Even metal outdoor furniture takes up more floor space than the indoor types.

With the emphasis on relaxed living, patios are usually stocked with more lounging furniture than a typical living room, and deck chairs, chaise longues, or sling chairs take up a great deal of floor area. Furthermore, the well-furnished patio compresses into its area much of the furniture and trappings of three indoor rooms—the kitchen, living room, and dining room. If the floor space is at all cramped, it doesn't take long for a patio to look as crowded as a furniture salesroom.

Another reason for generous scaling of the patio is the range of activity that takes place there. Ample space is needed for accommodating all the family plus your friends, for wheeling garden carts and loaded wheelbarrows, for free passage of three-wheeled children, for moving the furniture around to escape the sun. Patios are ideal game rooms, too, and there are few pieces of furniture equal to a ping-pong table for hogging floor area.

Not Too Big

Of course there are sensible limits. If too vast an area is converted to patio use, the effect can be quite depressing. An over-

A large, free-ranging house needs a generous-sized patio. This finely proportioned terrace actually emphasizes the house; and despite its size, it gives a protected, intimate feeling. Expansive paving provides a usable garden, rather than a "seeable" one. Communciation between garden and living room, dining room, kitchen and service room is free and easy.

Design: Douglas Baylis
Photo: Julius Shulman

Here is a small, private patio that is attached to a children's bedroom. As patios go, it is not so large—only 12-by-15-feet. But when this area is added to the 12-by-12-foot bedroom, it provides the room with a new dimension, a new horizon.

Design: Gordon Drake
Photo: Morley Baer

scaled patio may seem bleak and prairie-like. People retire to their patios to get refreshed, to escape the hard, cold surroundings they meet every day in business, at school, in the market. There is no pleasure in relaxing on a patio that reminds you of a parking lot or a playground.

Sometimes, however, the size of the lot itself is so generous that a large patio is unavoidable. With careful planning, it can be made "manageable" by breaking it up into areas that seem comfortable and right. Squares of plantings inset in paving will break up a monotonous surface; seat walls or raised beds can be used to put a stop to a seemingly limitless plane; baffle plantings or fencing can be used to divide the area into two or more functional spaces. The patio can be built on two levels, or the extra space can be devoted to a swimming pool.

If You Don't Have Space

If your space is quite limited, you have several recourses for making it comfortable and relaxing.

First requirement is to reduce the activities planned for the outdoor room in proportion to the available space. A freestanding barbecue, for example, would take precious floor space. A portable or a unit incorporated into the house chimney would do better; perhaps the barbecuing can be done in the service yard. Restrained use of plant materials will add charm to the patio, although overplanting will make it seem like a thicket, a hole in the jungle. Moderate-sized furniture will help. Lounging chairs, that sprawl over several square feet of floor, are likely to give a small patio a crowded feeling.

The small patio can be made to seem visually larger by various tricks of design. Stepped planting beds lead the eye upward and out of the confined area; tall, vertical screening gives it height; a slanting or curved outer boundary will suggest that there is more patio around the corner (even if there isn't) and a baffle fence can suggest the same discovery. Brick paving, with its small-scale, repetitive patterns, will seem to widen an area; a solid surface will also appear to give more space. But surfacings like tile or flagstone, with their emphatic mortar joints, will tend to make the room seem small.

What seems to be a generous-size patio on paper often turns out to be too small when you move the furniture onto it. It doesn't take much furniture to fill a patio. The assortment of typical pieces on the opposite page easily occupies 350 square feet—which is larger in area than many patios. Don't forget to allow room for garden vehicles, children's gear, and, of course, people.

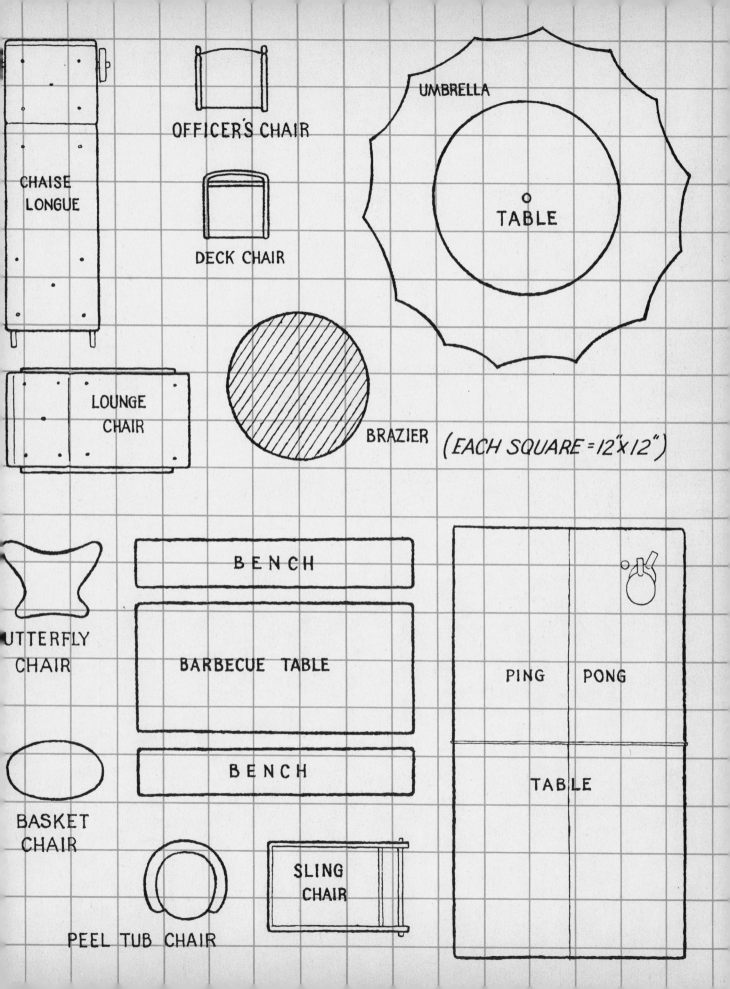

CHAISE LONGUE

OFFICER'S CHAIR

DECK CHAIR

UMBRELLA

TABLE

LOUNGE CHAIR

BRAZIER

(EACH SQUARE = 12"x 12")

BENCH

BARBECUE TABLE

BENCH

BUTTERFLY CHAIR

BASKET CHAIR

PEEL TUB CHAIR

SLING CHAIR

PING PONG

TABLE

HOW LARGE
SHOULD IT BE?

LEFT

Even a small outdoor living area takes on importance when it is tied in visually with the interior of the house. This example of a two-story window wall proves the point: When doors are open, you are outdoors, even if you are under the roof. Terrace continues outdoors at same level as floor of house.

Design: Lee Stuart Darrow
Photo: Ernest Braun

BELOW

On a small lot, it often takes some shrewd planning to create an outdoor living area that meets the requirements of an active family. In this small corner bordering the street, a curved plastic screen provides privacy and partial sun control, softens sharp angles of garden. Note curved bench in front of screen.

Design: Huettig and Schromm
Photo: Robert Cox

ABOVE

This large-scale patio is planned in "garden feet." The steps coming from the house are twice as wide and twice as long as they need be. The overhead trellis is generous and very expansive. The result is a patio with a free and easy look, ready to take care of any number of guests, and still in close relationship to the house.

Design: Lawrence Halprin
Photo: Philip Fein

RIGHT

When a house is ringed by hills, it takes a large-sized patio to hold its own with the surroundings. This large sunny terrace on the southeast side of the house provides a "transition zone" with two kinds of paving (exposed aggregate and old cobblestones) plus mounding plants growing in pockets.

Design: Rosalind Wheeler
Photo: Darrow M. Watt

Tie It In With the House

To serve you well, an outdoor living room should be firmly integrated with the house. If properly planned and placed, it has a beneficial effect upon life within the house itself.

Thus, a terrace outside the living room extends the living area beyond the walls of the house. Even when weather will not permit use of the outdoor area, it seems to make the inside room larger both visually and emotionally. A patio connected with a living room is a wide avenue of escape, removing all feeling of being closed in.

The patio can add a new dimension to other rooms as well. When a bedroom, den, or nursery opens on the outdoor living room, each gains a feeling of roominess. Activities can overflow into the patio. Out come the sewing machine, the children's paraphernalia; on summer nights, sleeping bags and cots appear for sleeping under the stars.

The benefits of a close relationship is a two-way affair. Since the patio is a combination living room, dining room, and kitchen, it gains in practical ways by being close to these rooms. Meals can be brought from the kitchen and dishes returned there with little effort and no spillage. Utensils can be borrowed for use at the barbecue. Linen and cutlery can be "lifted" from the dining room, company chairs from the living room.

Proximity to garage and workshop is also an advantage. Barbecue gear and firewood can easily be brought in, garden furniture can be stored and un-stored as occasion demands, and container plants can be whisked under cover when a nip is in the air.

Front, Side or Back?

Most patios are located in back of the house for various reasons. There is usually ample space, privacy and seclusion from the activities of the street are easily attained, and relationships with kitchen and dining room are usually smoother. However, this is not the only place to put a patio.

In Front of the House: Many very livable outdoor rooms have been built in front, between the house and the street. This takes careful planning to overcome the handicaps of the meager space usually assigned to this area by tradition and local setback ordinances. Such a patio is usually screened from the street, but it may be open to the approach from sidewalk to house. It makes an hospitable entrance, but it does not give full privacy.

As a practical matter, constructing a six-foot screen fence

An extension of an inside living area beyond the walls of the house, makes the inside room seem larger. A brick floor runs the full length of the house in back and carries out beyond the roof line of the porch, inviting full and free use of the porch for entertaining, dining, and loafing. Terrace beyond roof can be used for sun bathing.

Architects: Wurster, Bernardi, and Emmons
Landscape Architect: Thomas Church
Photo: Philip Fein

This patio at the side of the house, serves dining room and master bedroom. Door to bedroom, at left; dining room door at end of patio. Fence is redwood, 5 feet, 6 inches high—gives privacy from close neighbors. Patio near dining room facilitates its use for serving outdoor meals. Glass doors open onto the terrace.

Design: Gordon Drake
Photo: Morley Baer

across the front is usually prohibited in incorporated areas. Moreover, such a screen may mean that you will have to hide part of your house. It also requires finished craftsmanship and top-grade materials if it is to conform with general appearance of your house and neighborhood.

Alongside the House: A side yard is ordinarily an inauspicious site for a patio, at least within a city. Most city lots are so narrow that the space left open between the house and boundary line is barely wide enough for a walkway. Even if there is room, there is often no privacy, for the neighbor's windows may peer right down into the space.

Successful patios have been built in side yards, however, relying on carefully designed screen fencing for privacy and modifications in the house plan for elbow room. Using this space for a patio has some advantages: it converts to active use what is ordinarily waste space, and it frees the back yard for larger projects, such as a spacious garden or a generous play area for the children.

In rural or suburban areas where building sites are less constricted, a patio stretching down the side of the house can offer a maximum of livability. If it's covered over, it takes on the comfortable character of the old-fashioned screen porch that used to ring the house.

Pocket of an L or U?

Locating a patio in the pocket of an L- or U-shaped house has many advantages.

The protecting shoulder of the house shields the area from wind, neighbors, street sounds, and in some orientations, the hot sun. In mild climates, a paved patio of this type can be extremely useful as a secondary means of communicating between various rooms of the house—a secondary fresh-air hallway. Under ideal climatic conditions, perhaps a home need waste no valuable indoor space for hallways—let the space outdoors fulfill that function.

By facing the L- or U-shaped home towards or away from the sun, depending upon whether you wish to gather heat or discourage it, you can gain more positive weather control. In fact, the orientation of a U-shaped house must be approached with caution, for its shape is prone to intensify climatic extremes. The pocket of a west- or south-facing U can become unbearably hot in some localities. An overhead canopy often doesn't relieve the temperature because the arms of the U tend to retard free air

Bedroom looks out through glass wall to small paved terrace, a section of lawn, and garden pool. Terrace, on same floor level as bedroom, is protected by extended roof of house. Hill rises sharply behind curved retaining wall, insuring privacy.
Design: Cliff May
Photo: Maynard Parker

The early Western ranch house was often built right around its patio. This contemporary home in Los Angeles lets the exterior walls of three of its rooms create a small protected outdoor living area. This is view from the kitchen, looking across the patio into children's bedroom. Sliding glass doors, flush with the kitchen counter, allow easy serving of outdoor meals.
Design: Thornton Abell
Photo: Julius Shulman

circulation. Moreover, a U-shaped house faced uphill may catch and store the cold air that pours down the slope in winter.

Enclosed Court

A fully-enclosed patio, surrounded by the four walls of the house, has its peculiar advantages.

Strictly speaking, this type of patio abandons the benefits offered by the open-sided patio by turning away from the view, the sun, and the summer breezes. But in compensation, it offers absolute privacy—you can entertain or even sunbathe without observation—and where there is no view to begin with, it substitutes a pocket of light and color in the house. Roofed over, it makes a natural greenhouse, an unbeatable spot for growing specimen plants.

Although such a court has been known to home designers for many centuries, and was a popular form in Spanish California, it does not yield its best to the casual house planner. The secret is in making it large enough so air can circulate in it or drain out of it, and so the sun can reach into it at other hours than high noon. Without such forethought, a small enclosed court will be chilly as a cistern on cool days, icy as a deep freeze in winter, and a veritable oven on hot days.

RIGHT

Central court is a two-story-high "room" in this house. It is enclosed within the house walls, paved and planted like a garden, and entirely screen covered (also, a movable awning furnishes any degree of sun protection). This is the view from the master bedroom. You can just see into the family room, to right, past seated girl. Above her is second-story walkway.

Design: John Matthias
Photo: Ernest Braun

LEFT

Viewed from living room, glass-enclosed court brings sunlight and garden view into center of the house. This can be an ideal solution for a house on a small lot when people want privacy as well as openness and the benefits of a garden.

Design: Liddle & Jones
Photo: Hugh N. Stratford

ABOVE

Because it includes the entire lot in its patio, this house constantly is looking back on itself. Terrace of foot-square tile is laid directly on ground. Patio floor laid flush with house floor contributes a great deal to tying the house to the terrace. Glass windows used here could be turned into sliding doors for easy access to patio.

Design: John Bomberger
Photo: Phil Palmer

LEFT

Remodeled to include its own private patio, a master bedroom takes on a living room quality. High brick walls of the garden make practical the use of sliding glass wall. Original room was walled here with fixed window, flanked by French doors. Use of sliding doors ties the house into the patio area more completely. Curtains may be pulled to shut off patio.

Design: Cliff May
Photo: Julius Shulman

TIE IT IN WITH THE HOUSE

RIGHT

Here is an arrangement that eases its way from indoors to outdoors—living room to lanai to patio. Lanai, just outside living room, is former reed-covered patio which owners liked so much that they decided to give it a permanent roof. Patio was then extended further outward (see photo below).

BELOW

Floor of new garden room reaches on outdoors, making room and newly-extended patio continuous. Shutters like these intrigued owners while in Mediterranean area; they permit gentle breezes and can transform sunlight into a diffuse, romantic glow. Facade created by addition has elegantly simple form and finish.

Design: William F. Hempel
Photos: Ernest Braun

Fit It Into the Garden Plan

Although your patio area will be intended for social functions, family relaxation and as a general gathering-place, it is only one part of the whole house and garden arrangement and as such, it should be tied-in with these other elements if it is to fulfill its purpose.

As in the interior of your home, circulation through the patio is important. If it is necessary to pass through the patio area in order to reach other sections of the garden, such circulation should not disrupt play activities or people relaxing or conversing. If possible, provide a pathway around the outside of the patio to avoid traffic through the center of the space. Proper positioning of doors leading to the house and of gates to other garden activities will give you some control. If possible, place cooking facilities or game tables in corners or out of the usual lines of travel. Arrangement of furniture, location of planting boxes and the barbecue can be planned to facilitate easy and unencumbered passage.

Garden Work-Center

If you are addicted to gardening, the placement of the work spaces of the garden—the cold-frames, compost heap, topsoil bin, and pot storage—close to the patio may reduce much of the carrying to and fro. Separation will be necessary; but perhaps a simple wood baffle will do the job for you, screening off the workspace but not blocking the easy movement of loaded wheelbarrows.

Play Yard

With children, the patio might adjoin their very own area, separated by a low fence or a gate, so that at times they may be allowed to overflow onto the patio for games that need more space or for playing with wheeled toys. (See the chapter on the "Patio as Playground.")

Overflow Space

To provide for larger numbers of people than will normally gather on the patio, plan to use adjoining areas as supplementary overflow space.

A lawn area can be one of the most useful of overflow spaces. When not in use for this purpose, it serves as a handsome contrast to the pavement and as a vitalizing background for the

This terrace turns a corner surrounding the lawn area. Photo was taken shortly after a garden remodel which substituted permanent plant materials for seasonal plantings. Notice how garden feeling is retained by the use of square planting sections left at regular intervals in the bricks.

Design: Douglas Baylis

Same patio eight years later. The Monterey pines, tubbed bamboo, and other plantings have matured; the patio has become a tree-sheltered retreat with plenty of shade and a general atmosphere of privacy.

Photo: Joe Munroe

brighter colors of the house, patio furniture, and flowering plants. Selection of some of the tougher turfs will be a wise choice, for they will support heavy foot traffic for short periods with little or no damage.

As a second type of overflow space, perhaps you may decide on a smaller paved area surfaced with a more informal material. This secondary area might well be designed as the small courtyard from which branches a work area, the service area and even the children's play area. In this way, the paving is common to all and by simply moving a panel, or opening a gate, or rounding a hedge you transform this area into its working function during chore hours. By closing off the work spaces, the paving section adjoining the patio becomes available as overflow space. If you can arrange to have this courtyard close to the kitchen, perhaps here would be the most likely place to build your outdoor cooking facilities, store your movable barbecue, or raise herbs in boxes or pots.

As another possible overflow area, consider adding the equivalent of the entry to the house—a garden entry. A smaller central paved area where guests can be received without passing through the patio; where they might be diverted to the house to hang up coats and hats or be put to work. It would function as a neutral area between the house, the garden, and the street, leaving the house with greater privacy, and the patio with improved circulation. During a party crush, smaller groups might be diverted into this space.

Service Yard

Since most patios are equipped with lounging furniture, the storage of these pieces may present some problem to you. Try locating the service area near the patio so the former can double as storage space for your garden furniture. The garage could also be an appropriate place for this, if the doorway is large enough to permit the passage of wheeled lounges or heavy tables, that are often hard to lift and tilt sideways.

The service area will be a fine place to store surplus or rotating displays if you are a pot or box gardener, eliminating much heavy hauling. Because the service area will probably be fenced, it may be just the place handy to the patio into which you can lug the tender plants for protection on cold nights, and you will appreciate a short haul for this job.

If you are the owner of a portable barbecue unit, the service area will be just the place for parking it as well as its fuel and

An illustration of excellent circulation, these broad inviting brick steps lead to lawn area above main terrace. For small groups the terrace is large enough; overflow crowds can spread out easily over the whole garden. Note the service area in the back at the right is screened off by the use of a board fence. Terrace uses combined lawn and bricks.

Design: Tommy Tomsen
Photo: William Aplin

Although the usual case is to fit the patio into the garden plan, it is sometimes advisable to fit the garden plan to the patio. Here, the effect of a large paved patio is softened by large planting beds, change of materials (flagstone, lower right), and an irregular outline. Other ways to break up paved expanses include a change of level, free-standing fence panels.

Photo: Art Hupy

accessories. Here, too, you can broil the smokiest meats without distressing your guests. A good place for wood storage for the fire pit or outdoor heating fireplace.

Next to a Swimming Pool

If the patio adjoins a swimming pool, one of its probable requirements will be that of shelter from the wind and a place for dripping bathers to soak up the sun. Perhaps the barbecue can serve as additional heat by employing a combination cooking-heating design.

Keep in mind the reflective qualities of water and locate the pool so as not to cast a glare into the rooms of the house. In this case, perhaps the patio should lie in the shade of the house for added comfort during pool recess. Then, glare would no longer be a problem, for the pool would lie in a northerly direction. Instead, you would have the problem of drying the patio surface after a strenuous swimming session. Unless the water splashed from the pool or dripped from wet suits dries quickly, the patio may be uncomfortably damp, or watery footprints may be tracked into the house.

RIGHT

You feel comfortable alone on this terrace, yet it's spacious enough to accommodate 30 persons easily. Exposed aggregate paving is varied and minimized by brick insert squares, planting islands. Chosen for quick effect, birches, junipers, bamboo looked good as soon as planted.

Design: Marshall W. Perrow
Photo: Art Hupy

LOWER RIGHT

Circular patio, partially enclosed by a semi-circular screening fence, is terminus of a brick path that curves its way through the garden from a deck that adjoins the house. Mature Texas umbrella tree was already on the site; patio was built around it to take advantage of its generous shade. Setting is splendid for display of container plants. Large succulent in foreground is an aeonium.

Design: C. Jacques Hahn
J. Charles Hoffman
Photo: Marvin Rand

LEFT

From patio next to house, you can see the swimming pool, but there's a feeling of separation provided by the trellis and 40-foot-long bench. Burmese honeysuckle vines growing on vertical panels can be kept pruned back or allowed to grow unrestricted, depending on amount of screening desired.

Design: John Carmack
Photo: Phil Palmer

FIT IT INTO
THE GARDEN PLAN

LEFT

Patio before it was planted, showing how the curving lines of the raised beds repeat the dome-like crown and arching branches of large oak trees. They also follow contours of knoll on which house and garden are situated.

BELOW

Same patio, softened by planting. Evergreen background trees, such as stone pine, mark the garden boundary; with the passing of the years, they have grown large enough to create a skyline and a solid screen. Patio is actually a court, surrounded on all sides— by the house, guest house, and adobe garden walls.
Design: Geraldine Knight Scott

ABOVE

Curving terrace makes a pleasing design in this small garden. Path repeats the circular pattern of the concrete sitting area, and is also a curb for the flower beds.

Design: Arthur W. Erfeldt
Photo: Jeannette Grossman

RIGHT

The gardener who loves flowers and works hard at growing them can enjoy the fruits of his labor to the utmost by making them a part of the patio scheme. This garden patio belongs to a chrysanthemum hobbyist. Some plants are in pots, others are in the ground.

Photo: William Aplin

Detached Garden Shelters

The ever-present barbecue, influencer of outdoor living, started it all several years ago. From it and around it have grown shelters that provide outdoor living room for playing, eating, resting and hobby interests.

The cold fact that there are few localities where an unsheltered barbecue can be used all year was the key to the trend. The barbecue in a windy spot calls for wind breaks—and gets them. Provided with shelter from sun and rain, the barbecue is usable almost any weekend. Barbecue and outdoor fireplace, joined together in picture and thought, call for enclosure and get it.

As the idea of outdoor living rooms developed during the last couple of decades, the barbecue diminished in importance as a structural element. Dining became but one function of the room. More living of all kinds overflowed from the house to the garden and its shelter.

The garden shelter is often intended originally to be a secondary living area, but it nearly always becomes the most lived-in area of the house-garden complex.

Why a Detached Shelter?

There are important reasons to build a room detached from the house. By so doing, you can depart from the house's architectural style. Building materials which might clash with the house if the shelter were a part of it can be used with some freedom. Inexpensive construction materials and uncomplicated building methods are in order. Under these conditions, the enclosed garden shelter offers a happy opportunity for the owner to design and—if he so desires—build his own. Thousands of homeowners have proceeded without inhibitions to build a simple structure of 4-by-4 inch posts and a shed roof which serves as an extra room. The freestanding garden living structure also offers a solution to the homeowner who is cursed with a house which does not permit proper orientation of his patio area.

In a cool climate, a house whose patio exposure is on the cold north side offers a problem which is solved with relative ease by placing a shelter at the rear of the lot, facing the patio. The shelter becomes a south-facing garden living room that traps winter sun. The reverse of this situation is often the case in hot interior valleys

This spacious garden room has a marked casual, come-as-you-are atmosphere. Glass doors, open or closed, present a wide view; pitched roof lifts toward tree tops. Cooking and storage are around the fireplace. Floor is red concrete and woodwork is knotty pine. This room changes from garden retreat, to a children's room, or to a dining room with great ease.

Photo: Jerry Anson

Exterior of room above shows extensive lawn to the front, verbena and rose garden in the foreground. Buffet against the far wall holds dishes, decorations. The counter pulls away to reveal a sink. The owners think this shelter's pleasant effect on parties is due to its position in the garden—opening as it does on a spacious lawn.

and in the Southwest. There, if the patio side of your house faces into the summer sun, you can get the sun at your back by putting a shelter at the other side of the patio.

In hillside homes, or where the earth's contours won't let you have a patio associated with the house, such a shelter may be the only way to get an outdoor living area into the garden.

The shelter may serve the family's special interests and activities. It may take the form of swimming pool bath house, can include greenhouse facilities for the gardener, or special entertaining facilities like a smooth-surfaced dance floor.

Isolation from the house can be a·strong advantage. An imponderable, but very real sense of security and cozy comfort goes with sitting by a roaring fire in a small, weatherproof outdoor structure.

A separate shelter can keep playing children confined, especially during bad weather. It is a good place for high school age youngsters to entertain their friends.

Practical Considerations

If you are thinking of putting up an enclosed garden shelter, weigh its advantages against practical considerations. A close connection between the outdoor living room and the kitchen may be more advantageous than attempting to make the outdoor room independent of the house itself. Duplicating kitchen facilities can be very costly—and the washing of dishes and utensils, as well as the preparation of much of the food, may be better handled in the kitchen. A portable cart-like table can be used to transport food to and from the kitchen when outdoor facilities are incomplete.

One important point to remember is that the weather around your home must be studied before you can improve on it successfully. Sun and wind conditions should be known.

Outdoor shelters play an important role in increasing size of your total living space. Many homeowners with well-protected outdoor areas find that all need for a large inside living room vanishes when the outdoor living room is really usable. That fact is of special value if your house is small: through well-planned outdoor units, your garden house can be made to serve many of the functions of the large house.

Louvered doors to the right of this garden shelter open into a storage room 6 feet deep, 14 feet long. Other storage is back of the table tennis area. Roof is covered with corrugated plastic, rests on double 2 by 14-inch beams above storage areas; air space allows good circulation. Shelter is used for games, parties, and evening barbecues.
Design: Lloyd M. Bond
Balzhiser & Seder
Photo: Tom Burns, Jr.

In mild climate areas, it is possible to enjoy a simple shelter such as this all year long—provided there is wise orientation. This lanai-like shelter on the north side of an enclosed outdoor living area is backed up to a fence, and has a plastic roof that deflects the wind up and over.
Design: Sim Bruce Richards
Photo: Marvin Rand

DETACHED GARDEN SHELTERS

Shelter can make good sense for a hillside home, particularly where cramped quarters or small lot size limit size of house itself. The back of this structure is enclosed by a hedge of lush green laurel. Clear plastic covering protects furniture from rains and provides shade without blocking out too much light—an important consideration in areas where sunny weather is infrequent.

Design: Barbara V. Fealy
Photo: Tom Burns, Jr.

LEFT

Japanese teahouse is popular with adults and teen-agers alike. Shoji frames hold insect screening; this allows ventilation yet keeps out flies and night-time insects. Interior features a masonry firepit lined with sheet copper, with river-washed pebbles on the bottom. Rest a shallow pan full of glowing coals on the pebbles and guests can roast wieners, marshmallows.

Design: W. Bennett Covert
Photo: Robert C. Cleveland

LEFT

Pergola, although not a garden shelter in the true sense of the word, creates a pleasant and shady sitting and planting area around the edge of a sun-flooded patio. This spacious example, joined at one end to the house roof overhang, looks over the raised garden pool to the living and dining wing of the house.

Design: Jack Gibson
Photo: Ernest Braun

This shelter of natural stone from the Clear Lake area of eastern Washington is set away from the house, close to the shore of Lake Washington. Its facilities for lounging, cooking and eating are complete. Variations on this structure could include all-wood construction with openings screened; an all-year room with glass front and sides.
Photo: Charles R. Pearson

RIGHT

Summer house is enclosed top and sides by panels of glass fiber screening fastened to redwood frame. Beams over the passageway from house, left, extend across roof. Sliding doors are beyond grapevine, left center. Room's embellishments include metal fireplace, small pool, telephone jack.

Design: Robert Cornwall
Photo: Phil Palmer

The Patio as Playground

Your children will probably think that you have built your patio just for them.

In the opinion of a small child, the outdoor living room is obviously more useful to him than to his parents. During good weather, he uses it all day, but his parents spend only a few hours there in the evening and on week-ends. And when grownups do use it, they merely sit around, while he puts the patio to the full use for which it was designed.

The patio is the natural place to learn your wheels, to master tricycle, wagon, and skates. This is where you assemble wagon trains, set up housekeeping with orange crates, practice the arts that are forbidden indoors, such as, cooking with mud, throwing rubber balls, shooting water pistols, or wrestling with the dog. Above all, it is a sanctuary to be protected from the swarms of badmen, Indians, and dangerous beasts that infest the neighborhood.

When children outgrow these preoccupations, they can still monopolize the patio. Their activities become simpler, but they take up just as much space.

When planning a patio, you can anticipate your children's interests and provide for them long before the first brick is laid or square of concrete poured.

Some outdoor areas, such as this formal dining terrace, are used primarily by adults; however, the children's area is like an extension of the patio and is in full view (particularly desirable where there are toddler-age children). Capped grapestake fence at left screens small service area. When it is no longer needed, play area can easily become a second terrace.
Design: Arthur W. Erfeldt
Photo: Ernest Braun

Paving for Play

One simple requirement for a practical playground is to select a surfacing material that will not hamper the children's play or burden you with janitorial problems.

In general, a smooth surfacing will give more satisfaction than a rough paving, although it may not have the same aesthetic appeal (see page 62). Smooth paving is kinder to young knees, simpler to clean of finger paint, mud pies, and peanut butter, easier to negotiate on uncertain wheels. When the children reach high school, they can sprinkle cornmeal on the paving and slick it up for dancing.

Another requisite of a good play surface is quick drainage. A patio that dries quickly is a wonderful place to park the children after a rainy week indoors. A calculated slope to the paving will prevent water from standing and a smooth, even surface will keep it from puddling. Bricks-on-sand dry quickly. A wooden deck, built with the floor boards slightly separated, will dry swiftly.

A children's terrace permanently marked off for hopscotch, marbles, and shuffleboard. If you would prefer non-permanent lines, you can use a rubber base paint, which will eventually wear off, or you can make marks to indicate corners and intersections, filling in lines with chalk when necessary. Doors on right of terrace lead to inside play area; keep children away from other entrances.
Design: Smith & Williams
Photo: Julius Shulman

However, children are prone to drop treasures down the slots between boards; so allow for crawl space underneath to permit coins, comic books, candy, etc., to be retrieved.

Sand Boxes

A built-in sand box makes a canny addition to a patio. Built so it is water-tight and fitted with a drain, it can be converted later to a garden pool. Installed over garden soil, it can become a raised planting bed in later years. Or, if you simply leave out a square of paving, you can fill it in later to expand the patio paving. You won't mind the spilled sand—you can use it to lighten garden soil, or if you have a brick-on-sand patio, you can sweep it into the cracks.

Provisions for Games

If the patio area is large enough, you can paint the boundary lines of some games right on the pavement. Patterns for shuffleboard, hopscotch, or marbles can be etched into concrete in color with acid stain, or if you prefer to have them wear off eventually they can be painted on with rubber base paint. Foul lines of badminton, paddle tennis, or volley ball can be painted or etched on a larger patio; and sockets for the net poles can be cast into the paving at the time the patio is laid. If you don't like the idea of criss-crossing your patio with boundary lines, you can imbed little "benchmarks" to indicate corners and intersections, and chalk the lines in place whenever the area is to be used.

If your patio has a section of windowless wall, you can mount a basketball hoop on the eaves or on the roof (height to hoop: 9 feet). This will keep the teen-aged boy pre-occupied for hours.

Croquet: Official area is 36 by 72 feet, but it can be laid out in a much smaller space. Closely-cropped, leveled grass is the best surface. Rolled adobe or clay soil is often suitable; even a paved driveway can be used if stakes and wickets are inserted in blocks of wood. If game is played on the lawn, change position of wickets occasionally in deference to the turf.

Home Golf: Various forms of pocket-sized golf can be practiced on the lawn. *Clock Golf* requires a 12-foot, white circle (use powdered chalk or gypsum) with 12 points corresponding to the figures on a clock. A 4-by-4-inch hole is dug off center. Game is to hole-out from each point.

Tennis Games: Tennis itself requires plenty of space (see scale plan) and an elastic budget to prepare a truly suitable court. (Obtain specifications from the Asphalt Institute or Portland Cement

Taken separately, sand boxes and wading pools have always ranked high with the small fry of the household; team them up side by side, as in this intriguing example, and you have an unbeatable combination. This play area occupies a paved corner of a city lot. In later years, this area could become an attractive garden pool and planting bed.

Design: Ross Copeland
Photo: Art Hupy

Large back yard makes it possible to put play area at one end, with a generous expanse of lawn to mark it clearly as a separate domain. Tanbark is under gym set; other good surfaces would be firbark, sand, or smooth gravel ($\frac{1}{2}$ to $\frac{3}{4}$-inch size). Paved runways for tricycles go around the entire patio. "Freeways" like this are especially desirable if you live in a neighborhood with no sidewalks.

Design: Lawrence Halprin
Photo: Ernest Braun

Information Bureau; or read tennis pamphlet in the Spalding Athletic Library.) Although *Badminton* calls for a 20-by-44-foot field, it can be played in a smaller area. *Hand Tennis* is played without racquets on a 16-by-40-foot field, with the net set at 2 feet 4 inches. *Deck Tennis* uses rubber rings instead of balls and racquets, needs a 20-by-20-foot field. *Paddle Tennis* is played with paddles instead of racquets in a field 18-by-39-feet.

Bowling: The long-standing favorite, *Bowling on the Green*, requires a vast, level lawn 120 by 120 feet. A bowling substitute can be enjoyed with croquet balls. Set two stakes 30 to 40 feet apart and proceed as in horseshoes.

Handball: This strenuous game calls for an unbroken wall 16 feet high, 20 feet wide, and a playing area 20 by 34 feet. A double garage can sometimes be adapted.

Lawns for Scrimmaging

A sturdy lawn, flowing off the patio, will prove one of the most popular play areas for your children. Cooler than paving, it will attract them in summer. Softer than paving, it will be used for wrestling, rough-housing with the dog, practice scrimmaging. If you use it for net games, be sure to shift the net and foul lines frequently so players won't wear out turf in one or two places.

For greatest durability, plant a tough grass. One of the coarse fescues such as Alta (Kentucky 31) or Meadow will take plenty of foot traffic without any ill effects. Also, most seed companies feature mixtures made up of sturdy, easy-to-grow grass varieties. If you live in a warm-climate area, you might wish to try one of the Zoysias or Bermudas.

Private Patio for Children

If you don't relish the idea of sharing your patio too intimately with the children, you can plan one just for them. If the size of your lot permits it, set the play yard far enough away from the main one. Swings and bars will keep them busy; a surfacing such as firbark, sawdust, sand, or smooth gravel ($\frac{1}{2}$ to $\frac{3}{4}$-inch size) will cushion the inevitable falls. If you pave with soft materials, provide hard-surfaced garden paths for tricycle runs—otherwise all the rolling stock will turn up on the adults' patio. Provide shade, such as canvas or burlap, for sun protection.

For further information, see the *Sunset* Book, *Children's Rooms and Play Yards.*

Children are entitled to a place in the plans for patio development. When they outgrow the hopscotch and marble years, they become interested in action games that can often be fitted into the garden plan. A driveway or a level stretch of lawn will accommodate several games, such as those laid out at the right. Only a few people are likely to lay out a tennis court, but badminton or a telescoped version of croquet can be played in a reasonably small area.

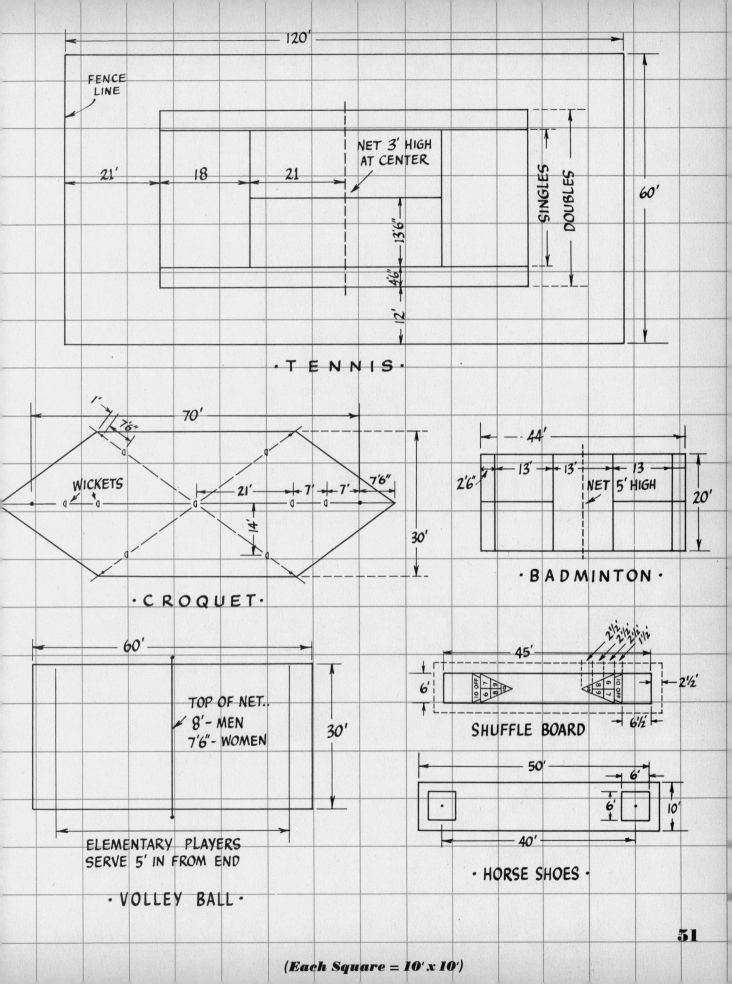

120'

FENCE LINE

21'

18

21

NET 3' HIGH AT CENTER

SINGLES

DOUBLES

60'

13'6"

4'6"

12'

· T E N N I S ·

1'

7'6"

70'

WICKETS

21'

7'

7'

7'6"

4'

30'

· C R O Q U E T ·

44'

13'

13'

13

2'6"

NET 5' HIGH

20'

· B A D M I N T O N ·

60'

TOP OF NET..
8' - MEN
7'6" - WOMEN

30'

ELEMENTARY PLAYERS
SERVE 5' IN FROM END

· VOLLEY BALL ·

45'

2½' 2½' 2½' 1½'

6'

10 OFF 7 9 8 6

8 6 9 7 10 OFF

2½'

6½'

SHUFFLE BOARD

50'

6'

6'

10'

40'

· HORSE SHOES ·

(Each Square = 10' x 10')

THE PATIO AS PLAYGROUND

LEFT

A combination of paving and lawn in children's area assures them space for their rolling stock to run on as well as a soft place to land at the end of a slide. The chain mesh fence is a good one for keeping small children confined, yet allowing them to survey the outside world. Plantings of daisies soften the institutional look of this type of fence.

Design: Paul Lazlo
Photo: Julius Shulman

RIGHT

Bedroom wing has two private patios, shared by three bedrooms. Master bedroom is to right of stuccoed dividing wall. The two children's bedrooms at left open to a concrete-surfaced play patio with an inviting built-in sand box.

Design: Thomas D. Church
Photo: Maynard L. Parker

RIGHT

A sloping lot offers excellent possibilities for setting up "two different worlds" in the back yard: one for children's play, the other for adult relaxing and entertaining. Children can be observed from the raised patio, yet the difference in levels permits them to play without being too conscious of adult proximity.

Design: Osmundson and Staley
Photo: Theodore Osmundson

LEFT

A play deck makes especially good sense in areas where rains are heavy, because of its ability to dry off in minutes. Steel pipe framework is popular for climbing, serves as structural background for planter that divides living area from play area. Swing set is anchored in concrete blocks set flush with top of decking.

Design: Robert Billsbrough Price
Photo: Chas. R. Pearson

Hillside Patios

A hillside patio presents both a challenge and an opportunity to its designer.

By opportunity, we refer to the potentialities for imaginative use of outdoor living space that becomes possible when you build on several levels, when you work a view into your plan, and when you design to fit the flowing contours of the hillside slope and the irregular boundaries that accompany today's hill lots.

By challenge, we refer to the formidable assortment of constructional problems that have to be solved before your patio can be put into operation.

If you have the good fortune of planning out your entire lot before the bulldozers go to work on it, you are free of many of the problems that beset the fellow who has bought a ready-built hillside home or who has hired his landscape architect after the house is built. Most competent architects will work out the garden plan for a hillside because the engineering factors involved are closely linked to the fate of the house itself, but occasionally, the problem of developing the land is left to the buyer.

Drainage

One of the first problems to work out is drainage. If you have a U-shaped house facing uphill, your central patio can be a perfect drainage sump for the water that slips down the hill behind you. To prevent this, slope the paving steeply away from the house, and at its edges run a line of drain tile to carry off the surface water.

Even though you may fill-in additional soil after the house is finished and though you slant this extra fill away from the house, you may have further work to do to protect your patio. Heavy equipment used during construction, the trampling of workmen around the house, and the piling of heavy loads of materials near the house will compress the original soil. This packing of the subsoil will tend to form an impervious layer through which the seep water will have difficulty passing. If you dump topsoil on top of this without taking the precaution of breaking up the compressed mass, water may simply seep through the relatively porous topsoil and lie stagnant, unable to permeate through the hardpan layer, causing settling, seepage through the walls of the house, failure of patio paving.

Overhead view of a patio that hangs on a steep hillside, yet manages to be level, private, comfortable, and protected from the winds. Terrace connects with both living and dining rooms, is opened up to the southern sun. Solid surface and fence design avoid feeling of dwelling on the edge of a cliff. Paving is concrete in redwood grids.
Design: Eckbo, Royston & Williams
Photo: Ron Partridge

Soil Retention

If it was necessary to cut deeply into the hillside to lodge the house firmly in place, it will be necessary to stabilize the raw soil to prevent sloughing off onto the patio surface. This can be done with plants, with terracing, with light wooden retainers held in place with stakes to delay the runoff of water; or, more ambitiously, by construction of a retaining wall or bulkhead. If the soil is one of the clay types that will absorb a great deal of water without allowing it to percolate through, small slides may occur. To prevent this, shave away the bank until the degree of the slope is lessened.

Air Drainage

A patio in a U- or L-shaped house, facing uphill presents another problem: cold air drainage.

Cold air, like water, will flow downhill and collect in hollows and low places where it will remain until the sun disperses it. An improperly oriented hillside patio will collect this cold air to the intense discomfort of the human beings and plant life in the patio.

Like water, cold air can also be diverted or dammed. One method to shield your patio is to plant a solid mass of shrubs or to build a fence part way up the bank to divert the flow of cold air. Another method is to plant or build a screen that will detour prevailing winds past your patio to siphon out cold air that may be lodged there. Or you can leave an opening or a gate on the downside to release the trapped air.

Trees

If your site is fortunately equipped with trees that are worth saving, a very important precaution is in order when you begin grading the site for the patio.

If you permit the newly leveled soil to be piled around the tree, the tree may suffocate. Tree roots need a loose and porous soil to allow the waste gases generated in the process of assimilation to find their way upward. When it is necessary to change the grade around the tree, provide a drain line below the level of the original soil, lay down several inches of gravel or loose stones over the root areas, and finally, build a well about the trunk.

It may also be necessary to provide vertical stacks of drain tile from the original grade to the new to be used as funnels for apply-

This house and its patio deck meet the three-dimensional requirements of building on a sloping lot. House appears to sit on the deck, creates the effect that deck runs continuously through house. Large deck area is adjacent to the kitchen and entertaining. Wide, counter-like sill tends to keep occupants back from deck edge.

Design: Fred Langhorst
Photo: Ernest Braun

Pier and post construction was used to support the house and deck pictured and described above. Concrete foundation anchors house on the uphill side. Deck drains directly to the hill where water dumps into the concrete-lined drain visible at left, under the house.

Design: Fred Langhorst
Photo: Ernest Braun

ing plant food to the roots. These can be arranged in a circle around the trunk about 8 feet apart.

Visual Element

Fitting a patio into a hillside sometimes involves subtle feelings of security, quite apart from the hard engineering factors involved.

A main requirement for a patio is a level space big enough for games and entertaining with some safeguards against a child's tumbling down the slope. To create this level space, it will be necessary to cut into the hillside or to add earth to the slope, or to both cut and fill. Or, another treatment might be to construct a deck, supported on posts. If too much soil is removed in cutting away the hill, the resulting slopes may well appear so insecure that the level area cannot be enjoyed. On the other hand, too large and steep a fill may suggest the possibility of the patio's sliding down the hillside. With the deck, supporting posts that do not appear to be heavy enough to support the weight of the structure will also appear much too precarious for comfort. The net result is that sometimes it is necessary to modify the requirements for level space to prevent the appearance of insecurity in the hillside garden.

For more ideas, see the *Sunset* Book, *Hillside Homes*.

Living, dining, kitchen areas all open out on this deck, planned to substitute for the terrace of a one-story house. Because it is better protected than most terraces, the deck serves to extend the living of the house every month of the year. Deck faces east over wide-open view of lake. Steps at the end of deck lead easily to garden below.

Design: John I. Mattson
Photo: Chas. R. Pearson

LEFT

This house solves the problem of its location on a Washington lake hillside with deck and terrace outdoor living areas. Upper deck gives feeling of stability and safety to large living room glass wall, provides lounge. Deck is for adults; children play within easy view on the terrace below. Lighting for deck is under eaves; terrace lights are in the deck overhang.

Design: Young & Richardson,
Carleton & Detlie
Photo: Chas. R. Pearson

RIGHT

Deck off the dining room is the main outdoor play area for the family which lives in this steep hillside residence. There is room for the small daughter to ride her tricycle in and out of the house here, and the wire and 2-by-4 railing adds to safety for children. A table and portable barbecue is often set up for outdoor meals.

Design: Worley K. Wong
Photo: Philip Fein.

HILLSIDE PATIOS

Sometimes the best location for the outdoor living area of a hillside home is away from the house rather than immediately adjacent to it. This grassy circular terrace resulted from leveling of a slope below the house. Low stone wall adds eye appeal as well as safety. Large firepit makes a natural gathering place, can be used for wiener roasts.

Design: Cash Beardsley
Photo: Chas. R. Pearson

Where owners wish to dine frequently out-of-doors, a small, intimate terrace with hillside view can be a pleasant and handsome solution. Kitchen and dining room open directly onto round terrace. Curved retaining wall of stone lends a dramatic flourish and is handy for informal seating.

Design: Lawrence and Hazen
Photo: Art Hupy

Extra dividends of this deck are magnificent views over San Francisco Bay, living area convenient to planting accents from the tops of neighbor's trees. Deck flooring is 2-by-6-inch redwood, spaced 1/4-inch apart, with ends and edges leveled to prevent splinters. Built-in seats at each side. Down stairway leads off at right.

Design: George Rockrise
Photo: Ernest Braun

The detailing on this deck gives it a strong, horizontal design. Note corners extending beyond last supporting posts, and the 2-by-19-inch handrail which lies flat. Pier support proved as strong as cantilevering in this deck installation. The planting around the base of the posts and bracing is entirely of California natives.

Design: Smith and Williams
Photo: Julius Shulman

This deck, pictured in profile above, is only seven feet wide, though it suggests a feeling of larger outdoor space. The wide board at the end is for seating. The narrow 1-foot side boards are for setting food and drink. The deck floor is of 2 by 6's, spaced ⅜-inch apart to allow for expansion and contraction of wood, drainage, circulation.

Design: Smith and Williams
Photo: Julius Shulman

Pavements for Patios

When you choose a paving material for your patio, you will find there are several excellent surfacings to select from. Bricks, tile, concrete, asphalt, flagstones, or adobe blocks are all fine, durable materials—if used in the right place and competently installed.

Each of these materials has shortcomings as well as virtues, however, and the chances are that no one surfacing will completely satisfy your expectations.

When you are weighing the pros and cons of the various paving materials, check them against standards such as those that follow.

Paving Checklist

1. An ideal pavement should have a pleasing surface texture: one that doesn't glare, that is non-skid. A soft-*appearing* texture is more appealing than one that looks hard and slick.

2. Patio paving should be reasonably easy to take care of. Stains from food, mud, or children's play should be removable without drastic action. The paving shouldn't require frequent overhauling.

3. The surface should level off smoothly for swift drainage, for easy movement of furniture, for easy dancing, and for uninterrupted passage of juvenile vehicular traffic.

4. The material should harmonize with the construction materials used in the house and garden structure, and it should harmonize with the textures and tones of garden plantings.

5. If expense is a consideration, the surfacing should be one that can be put in place at reasonable cost. The range of paving costs may run from about 10c a square foot for asphalt (owner-applied) to several dollars a square foot for flagstones, the aristocrats of paving materials. Somewhere inside this spread is the pavement that will suit your needs and your bankroll.

6. Good paving should be weather-resistant. It shouldn't buckle, sag, or crack in cold weather; melt in hot spells; or get so warm underfoot in summer that it is uncomfortable to walk on. If you want to store the day's heat, you would need one kind of paving; if you wish to dispel it, you would choose another.

7. If you want to put it down with your good right arm, you will want to know whether this is possible. Some types are easily put in place, others call for heavy machinery.

Bricks make an adaptable surfacing for patios. Warm red tones blend well with structural materials of house, colors of garden. In winter, when garden is often drab, brick paving contributes a cheery color. Easily put in place by an amateur. Can be laid in great variety of patterns (this is basket weave); can be obtained in several styles and surface textures.
Design: Eckbo, Royston & Williams
Photo: Morley Baer

Concrete and gravel are two favorite materials for patios; they can be made to work together effectively. Here, modular panels of dichondra act as green transitions between gravel and concrete paving. Notice how grid pattern of header boards marches rhythmically back from the raised rose bed to the house.
Design: Schuyler Reed Hafely
Photo: Morley Baer

Which Paving is Best?

If you were to match up the available paving materials against this checklist, you would come out with something like this:

Bricks

Bricks provide a pleasing, non-glare, non-skid surface. They are easy to put down yourself and without crippling cost. Their colors and textures and patterns blend with almost any structural material and look at ease in a garden surrounding. The warm red tone is a welcome sight in winter, when the garden is dead and drab. Disadvantages: some bricks disintegrate in freezing winter, they are hard to clean, they are a bit rough and irregular for dancing or sliding furniture, and they will heave up in frost areas.

Concrete

Concrete can be poured in place in modest squares by an amateur, and it is not expensive if owner-handled. It offers a choice of several finishes, many colors, and various textures, from slick to pebbly. With mechanical assistance, it can be swiftly laid in place. Disadvantages: some finishes are cold and commercial looking; if not properly applied, concrete will disintegrate; it is difficult to color evenly and permanently.

Asphalt

Asphalt paving is inexpensive, and if properly applied over a durable base, should do as well as any garden paving. It can be put down in small amounts by an amateur, but large areas call for professional application to achieve smooth, level surfaces without "bird baths." Disadvantages: some mixtures will fray at the edges, soften in warm weather and show wheel tracks and furniture marks. Asphalt stores heat, is good for a cool patio; impossible for a hot one.

Flagstones

Probably the most expensive of patio surfacings, flagstones give unmatched permanence if properly laid. In certain localities, they match the rugged terrain; in others they look inappropriate, imported. Disadvantages: to some people, they seem cold and quarry-like; their colors and random patterns are hard to work into subdued results.

Tiles

Tiles give a smooth, dressy look to a patio; are particularly suited to one that runs indoors. They are expensive, hard for an

TOP LEFT

Asphalt probably offers the patio builder the most paving for his money. Appearance is good if contrasting brick or wood borders, plants or concrete are used. Asphalt does not reflect heat or light, and it is easy to handle in small quantities. In a warm climate, asphalt gets hot underfoot, may sag or crack with soil movement. Sharp objects leave dents in it and weeds may come through.

Photo: Mason Weymouth

TOP RIGHT

Tile—of patio or quarry type—is a sophisticated, finished-looking surface. But cost is high. Tile is generally conceded all the advantages of concrete and then some. Its ceramic surface is good-looking, and you can get a range of color and abrasive qualities. Waxed, it is good for dancing. Some homeowners dislike its slick look which may add to the formality of the patio.

Photo: Mason Weymouth

LOWER LEFT

Adobe has the rich, warm texture of the earth from which it is made. The informal, soft-looking adobe patio floor throws no glare or reflection—and it provides an amazingly flattering background for plant and flower colors. Cost is about the same as brick in most locales. Here, in Sunset's patio, dichondra planted between adobe bricks lends a softening effect.

Photo: Darrow M. Watt

LOWER RIGHT

Flagstone patio surfaces often outlast the houses to which they are appended. Harder types survive where brick fails in the cold. Its landscaping value is highest in heavily wooded areas, and where it is applied in large scale. A good installation calls for master craftsmanship and artistic matching of pieces. Cost is very high. Objections: It is cold, hard in appearance. Unless you are a top amateur mason, it's hard to lay.

Photo: Mason Weymouth

amateur to lay without staining, but suave and smooth in the hands of a skilled tilesetter.

Adobe Blocks

Blocks of stabilized adobe are easily and quickly laid in place. If they contain an adequate amount of asphaltic stabilizer, they last indefinitely. Limitations: They tend to crumble at the edges; like asphalt, they store up heat and restrict their value to cooler patios. They need a level bed, for they fracture readily.

Soft Materials

Sometimes, soft materials of temporary or secondary nature have a place in patio paving. Gravel, hill-run aggregates, tanbark, crushed brick—any of these can be used with smart effect to supplement permanently paved surfaces.

Ways of using and applying these materials, and also those listed above, are fully discussed in a Sunset Book entitled *How to Build Walls, Walks, and Patio Floors.*

BELOW

Regions with abundant natural supplies of certain kinds of rock give landscapers some out-of-the-ordinary choices in paving materials. This terrace, in Salt Lake City, is paved with hard sandstone in buff, yellow, and pink hues. Same stone is used for pool at far end, comprised of sandstone of various thicknesses stacked against the wall. Water piped from behind flows between slabs into pool.

Design: Leon Frehner
Photo: Samson B. Knoll

PAVEMENTS FOR PATIOS

Laid side by side, these brick dividers add contrast and color to a patio floor. A handsome variation which uses fewer bricks is to lay bricks end to end between the concrete squares. Brick used in ways such as this can be especially effective in breaking up the monotony of a large paved area. It can also tie in with more brick; here, for instance, notice the raised bed three bricks high.

Design: Lloyd Bond
Photo: Tom Burns, Jr.

Here, pebbles were carefully laid following a scale drawing previously made to show the pattern. A 1½-inch layer of concrete went directly on top of the existing smooth concrete. Brown and green polished pebbles of uniform size were used. Light grid of 1 by 1-inch dividers is in good scale (surfaced, about ⅝ inch).

Design: Georg Hoy
Photo: Darrow M. Watt

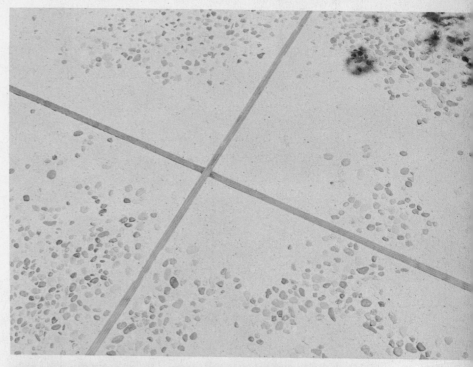

Fine gravel is an excellent paving for secondary patio areas. Over a rocky fill base, it holds up well, drains off moisture easily. If it is kept rolled and packed, gravel forms a pleasingly textured, nondusty surface. Best paving gravel size is about ½ inch in diameter. To keep weeds out of gravel and gravel out of flower beds, use a relatively thin layer, raked, tamped or rolled hard while it is moist.

Photo: Philip Fein

Fences and Walls for Privacy

In today's outdoor living scheme, the fence has ceased to be a mere boundary marker or a barrier against intruders. With family living extending to the lot line, the fence has now become another wall of the house; and as such it has taken on new patterns, new ways of construction to fit its new prominence.

The six-foot screen fence is often an absolute necessity to a house that opens its heart to the outdoors. Without this protection the family may be denied the privacy needed for full enjoyment of outdoor living. In addition, the fence serves as the horizon or backdrop for the garden when viewed from the house.

The fence builder has a great variety of fencing styles from which to choose. According to his tastes or the design of his house, he can select a solid fence made of boards, plywood sheets, or plastic panels; he can pick out a partly open variety built of alternating boards, woven strips, slats, or pickets. He can select his own degree of privacy, from complete (board fence), through partial (louver), to none whatsoever (picket). He can also choose the degree of weather protection. For wind shelter, he can erect a slat fence, a glass wall, or a baffle-capped variety; for wind attraction, he can slant a vertical louver to trap the merest breath of summer coolness. He can paint the fence to attract the sun or repel it; or he can color it to match the house, trim, or to contrast with garden plantings.

Many homeowners successfully build their own fences, for this is not difficult to do. The main chore is the post setting—and sometimes this is a task well worth passing along to a contractor. Once the posts are in place, however, the rest of the fence is easily assembled. The time required varies according to the kind of fence. A crew can assemble a 200-foot basket weave in an hour or two; but they may need a day or two to nail on the 1000 slats needed for the same length of grapestake.

The skilled handyman can also build a masonry wall to serve a screening function. Walls of brick, adobe blocks or concrete block are not beyond the capacity of the average week-end mason. Stonework, however, exacts genuine craftsmanship; and poured concrete takes equipment and elaborate forming and staging. City building inspectors worry more about walls than about fences and they establish more painstaking standards for the former.

For further details on fences or walls, see the *Sunset* Books on these subjects.

Fence that encloses this outdoor room is made of plastic screen panels, which alternate with modules of bamboo. Plastic provides restful lighting, keeps out all wind whereas some gets through the bamboo. Screen consists of regular window screen sealed in a "sandwich" of translucent plastic. Silhouettes of plants behind screen have the subtlety of a Japanese print.

Design: John Carmack
Photo: Phil Palmer

Staggered grapestakes fence and brick retaining wall actually form the fourth wall of the living room in this house. The vertical members of fence add pattern, give additional privacy from the street. Note barbecue grill included in brick wall at lower right. Trailing plants on retaining wall, erect plants against grapestakes soften hard lines of walls.

Photo: Morley Baer

FENCES AND WALLS FOR PRIVACY

West end of this Honolulu lanai has wall of vertical redwood louvers. In the full-open position, louvers admit maximum amounts of sun and air, emphasize lanai's closeness to the garden. Control bar near floor (see photo at bottom of page) operates louvers.

Design: Lemmon, Freeth, and Haines
Photo: R. Wenkam

When louvers are in closed position, they form a solid wall to protect the lanai from westerly wind or rain or a too-bright late afternoon sun. Although wall appears to be perfectly flat in first glance at photo, each redwood board is actually at a slight angle from the floor. Edges of boards overlap neighboring pieces by a fraction of an inch, forming complete closure.

Photo: R. Wenkam

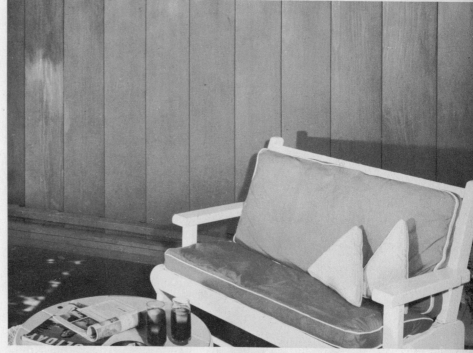

Each louver is hinged to control bar at one corner. Louvers may also be adjusted by moving any panel: others take same position. The 2-inch by 12-inch panels pivot on brass rods top and bottom.

Photo: R. Wenkam

Roofs That Invite the Sun

Some patios beg for sun. If located on a north side, where the sun never enters, or on an eastern side where only the morning sun intervenes, or if situated in a group of trees that provide perpetual shade, the patio needs every spark of sunlight that it can capture.

In such a situation, a patio may be better off with no sheltering roof. Sometimes, an open-work roof is needed to convey the feeling of protection without sacrifice of light. In damp climates, a solid but transparent roof may be in order.

Egg-Crate Overheads

You can get a small degree of sun conditioning with overhead "egg-crate" grids—slight shade, protection from slanting, direct rays in morning or late afternoon and a little wind deflection. The effect of such open work overhead is probably more psychological than protective. Grids do not interfere with the free flow of air and sun, yet they create the sensation of shelter when you stand or sit under them. They can also be used to smooth over the usually sharp break between indoor and outdoor living areas.

Grids are often used to create shadow patterns in a patio. As the sun moves across the sky, the gridwork casts shadows of varying size and shape on the surface below.

Lattice and Lath

Direct rays of the sun can also be filtered through any of various overhead lattice or lath structures—are a lively landscaping device—and they show how lattice work breaks up the sun's hottest rays.

Lath roofs break the force of winds without stopping vertical air circulation. They make the sheltered area cooler in summer, warmer in winter, and provide excellent shelter for more delicate plants.

Of course, climbing vines can be trained on either lath or grid shelters to increase control of summer sun.

This completely roofless room is carved into the steep, craggy north slope of Camelback Mountain, near Scottsdale, Arizona. Green planting around the perimeter contrasts with the severity of desert growth, relieves the sun's glare, and softens rocky contours. Yet all this was accomplished without shutting out any of the natural things that made owners choose the site in the first place.
Photo: Clyde Childress

Egg-crate roofing blocks off late rays of afternoon sun, creates strong shadow patterns, and lets full sun into area that needs it. Structure fulfills incidental function of giving the feeling of shelter without excluding the sun. If properly designed, egg-crates can also break up wind. May be used as arbor for deciduous vines if summer sun is too hot.
Photo: M. Halberstadt

Screen

You can combine copper or galvanized flyscreen with grid or lattice or use it alone for moderate shelter. Screen overheads provide real protection from falling twigs and leaves. In locales where mosquitoes and other flying insects are a problem, screen enclosure is often a must for comfortable outdoor activity.

Like gridwork, screen affords little real shelter from the sun's rays even though it creates the sensation of shelter. Air circulates freely in a screened area, though moving air is slowed as it passes through the rather tight mesh.

You can support screen over a considerable overhead area with heavy galvanized or copper wire. Pull the wire tight and apply screen over it.

Lightweight box beams and reed screen add 6 feet to existing roof overhang over this south-facing glass wall, for a total of 11 feet of shading width that keeps out most of low spring sun's rays. No posts obstruct the view or interfere with patio activities. Several variables affect the length and load of such a cantilever; get the advice of an architect or engineer and the approval of your building inspector.

Photo: Bert Goldrath

Canvas Webbing

Another effective dual-purpose roof that bars some of the sun's heat, yet admits light on dark days, can be made of strips of heavy canvas. Canvas should be woven in basketweave fashion on a rigid frame as illustrated. You can achieve a fairly dense shade with canvas strips without the heavy structure necessary if lath or grids were used to deliver similar shade.

Glass and Plastic

Where there are more cool, misty days in a year than hot ones, a shelter of glass or translucent plastic makes good sense.

Wire glass and plastic roofs cost about the same in most cases. Both provide shelter yet permit solar light and heat to enter unimpeded. If the patio shelter is against the house, they do not cut light off from house windows. Both are available in an assortment of colors.

Plastic is easier to install than glass. It can be sawed with an ordinary cross-cut saw and attached with special nails. Some types of plastic may fade or buckle under certain conditions or if applied improperly. If you decide to install a translucent shelter roof, discuss the pros and cons of each with the building inspector or a dealer who sells and installs both materials.

Addition of translucent plastic roof made this large deck usable more months of the year. Deck is now protected from sun, but isn't dark. Plastic can be sawed with ordinary crosscut saw, nailed into place with special nails. Sheets come in many colors, sizes, and weights. This overhead was prefabricated, then erected on the site in two days.

Photo: Joe Munroe

ROOFS THAT INVITE THE SUN

Miniature louver metal screen appears translucent when viewed from below, yet it cuts out much of sun's heat, little light. Cost is a little higher than copper flyscreen. Louver screen comes in rolls, works best in panels as pictured at left. It is treated with a chemical to make surface resistant to salt air. Screen may make whistling sound in high wind.

Photo: Ron Partridge

Simple lath roof, a perennial favorite, is an easy hammer-and-saw job for the average home-owner. "Lath" is actually 2 by 2-inch lumber, spaced about 2 inches apart, supported on molding above windows and by a 2 by 10-inch beam. Posts are two 2 by 6's spaced 2 inches apart.

Photo: Robert Hamill

ROOFS THAT
INVITE THE SUN

Woven canvas strips cast a changing shadow pattern on the living area below. Basket weave assures ventilation, sun below, yet it offers shelter from the hottest rays. Woven canvas strips are excellent for awnings in windy areas—they have considerably less tendency to catch high winds sail-fashion than regular solid canvas awnings.

Photo: Jerry A. Anson

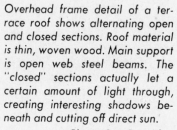

Overhead frame detail of a terrace roof shows alternating open and closed sections. Roof material is thin, woven wood. Main support is open web steel beams. The "closed" sections actually let a certain amount of light through, creating interesting shadows beneath and cutting off direct sun.

Photo: Ron Partridge

Roofs That Keep the Sun at Bay

Where summers are hot, the prerequisites of patio comfort are shade and plenty of freely circulating air.

In milder climates, many a south or west-facing patio makes the same demands for comfort.

Open, roofed shelter can be tied into the house structure or it can stand free of it in the patio. The West's early Spanish settlers and the Americans who followed them favored shelter that was a part of their homes: wide, deep porches often surrounded the entire house.

Porches

Porches are still an admirable defense from the sun, especially when patio paving extends beyond the porch visor. Living naturally tends to flow out of the house to the porch and right out on the patio, depending on weather conditions. The conveniences of the house are close at hand when you are on the porch: conversely, the outdoors shelter is so close to indoors that you can take advantage of it, with the least possible inconvenience.

When the weather turns bad, you can pull outdoor furniture in out of the rain; during winter, you can keep furniture there for use on occasional warm days.

Since the porch is a continuance of the house, you may want to roof it in the same material, and retain house building style. A porch that matches its house makes the house look and feel bigger, and the solid, permanent roofing material used is generally a better heat insulator than lighter, temporary roofing. Shingles or shakes of wood or asphalt composition, tar and gravel, tile, or asphalt rolls are good, standard roof materials.

Reflective Roofs

If you want to reflect some of the heat that strikes your porch roof, use shiny or white materials that will bounce some of the sun's heat back to the sky. Good materials for this purpose are: aluminum shingles, galvanized iron or aluminum in either corrugated or flat sheets, or crushed white dolomite substituted for gravel in a tar-and-gravel installation. It's not a good idea to use a reflective porch roof under second story windows because of reflected heat and glare.

Here, style and building materials of the house were used to tie house and outdoor room together architecturally and provide large, sheltered space. Woven redwood screen breaks the wind, keeps sun out of area in late afternoon. Paving extends beyond the roof-line, makes covered patio look and feel larger than it actually is.

Design: Pietro Belluschi
Photo: Ron Partridge

Indoor-outdoor living room is just outside house living room, provides friendly gathering place between outdoor pool and play area. Here, the house roof and structural design were extended over a concrete terrace to create a large room between house and outdoors. Decorations and furnishings were selected to add to indoor-outdoor transitional effect.

Design: Burton A. Schutt
Photo: Harry H. Baskerville, Jr.

In planning a porch, try to strike a balance in proportion between letting too much sun into the house and shutting off too much view. For instance, if the porch roof slopes to a level lower than eye level inside the house, you will have the same feeling of annoyance you get trying to look under the brim of a hat turned too low.

Extension of the porch floor beyond post and roof line increases the apparent size of the porch beyond actual measurements.

Freestanding Shelters

Freestanding shelters and lighter, lean-to, awning structures attached to the house have some of the advantages of the porch and others that are their own. They can often be constructed less expensively than a porch because the builder is not wedded to house style and structural materials. Size does not have to be in proportion to that of the house, and in the case of freestanding shelters, all four walls can be open to circulating air. Orientation is also a lesser problem in freestanding shelters.

The design of a patio shelter often is more sensitive to the demands of its owner than the design of the house proper. If you plan such a shelter, give careful consideration to sun, wind, the need for privacy and special activities dependent upon the shelter. As examples on these pages indicate, there are few standard solutions to shelter needs. Each tends to be the natural result of the owners' needs in relation to site, house and climate.

Canvas

There are standard roof materials for patio shelters. Those mentioned above can be used, of course. Most awning and separate garden shelters use lighter roof materials, however. Canvas is foremost of these. Canvas can be sewed in a shape to fit over a permanent frame. Grommets (large, metal eyelets) at the corners, and where the canvas meets the rafters, will help keep it in position. Grommets have to be died into canvas. Many canvas dealers will lend you grommet dies.

You can also stretch canvas over a ridge pole to make a gable-like shelter. Corners are hooked with grommets over nails, and edges are snapped to a tight guy-wire with spring snaps.

Gay, bright-topped canvas pavilion has stripes of saran shade cloth (for shade pattern and view of tree top), spreads shade around slim young tree. Demountable frame for laced canvas is electrical conduit on four pipe uprights. It has 7-foot hole in center for tree, no center post, and spans 20 feet. With no right angles or level members, it fits outdoor area of any shape.

Design: Walter Houk
Photo: Darrow M. Watt

Canvas is hard to beat as a shade-providing shelter for outdoor living. In this example, canvas is laced on pipe frame set in concrete. It shades windows and most of terrace from high sun, keeps even the early morning sun away from windows in house. Canvas is durable and relatively inexpensive, comes in almost every color of the rainbow.

Photo: Frank L. Gaynor

Another canvas-topped shelter for patio use is a circus-like tent. It can be anchored around a tree in the patio whose foliage is not broad enough for shade or shelter; or, use any center pole. The canvas is steadied by guy-ropes attached to stakes in the ground.

Support or framing for canvas shelters need not be as bulky as that necessary for a roof constructed of wood and practically any rigid roofing material. It requires less framing—and can be used for greater rafter-less spans—than burlap.

Though support for overhead canvas roofs is usually less complicated than for most other overheads, it must be fairly sturdy and firmly anchored. A broad expanse of canvas takes on all the qualities of a sail in a high wind. Without proper support, your awning may take off over neighboring yards or wrap itself around the barbecue.

One distinct advantage of canvas is the wide range of colors in which it is available. You can get vat-dyed or factory-painted canvas in practically every color of the rainbow. The factory-painted type is generally more color-fast than vat-dyed canvas. Use factory-painted material if the shelter roof is not to be folded very often, vat-dyed duck for often-collapsed shelter roofs.

Good quality canvas, properly installed, will withstand strong winds and will shed rain water. Its tightly woven texture retards air movement.

Burlap

Burlap is also a good awning material. It is not as tough and durable as canvas, but its open weave makes for better ventilation in any fairly large covered shelter. It also serves as a filter to the sun's rays, admitting light that canvas blocks off entirely. Use grommets on the heaviest burlap and lace it to a wood or metal frame with awning twine. Burlap will not shed a summer shower.

Plastic Sheeting

New plastic awning materials are constantly being developed. Performance and characteristics of these cloths vary so widely that no flat statement about their value would hold true in all cases. They are generally light, strong and more expensive than a similar grade of canvas. Talk plastics with a local awning dealer to find out how different cloths perform under local conditions.

Shady side yard terrace suggests how you might create a similar cool spot in any 10-foot side yard. Dwarf trees and burlap, stretched taut between extensions to roof rafters, provide shade and privacy from neighbors. Notice the already-generous overhang on this house, located in Phoenix, Arizona.

Design: Fred Griffen
Photo: Frank Gaynor

Roofs That Meet the Sun Half Way

Ideal overhead for the patio is one that is adjustable to match the moods of the weather and the seasons, that can be opened to lure a reluctant sun or capture a needed breeze; or that can be closed to exclude a merciless sun, shut off a downdraft, or shelter you from a shower. When the sun deserts you for the winter, you can remove the patio cover and store it away for the next season.

Adjustability is particularly desirable if your patio is a small one or is completely covered by an overhead. Here you can't win by committing yourself to solid over-head shelter or by leaving your patio wide open to the sky. One day you want a roof over your head; the next, you'll probably want wide open space. An adjustable overhead is also sometimes welcome when a patio is located next to a picture window, because the shelter that shades the patio may cut down the sunlight in the house to an uncomfortable degree.

No perfectly adjustable overhead has been developed, but there are some good compromises. Singly or in combination, they turn back many of weather's troublesome characteristics.

Sliding Canvas

Canvas probably provides the most versatile of overhead shelters. You can sew rings or spring snaps to a large piece of canvas, slip the rings over wire stretched at equal intervals on a wood or metal frame and slide the resulting awning back and forth to meet changing weather conditions. If the awning position is seldom changed, you can push it back and forth by hand; but ropes and pulleys make it a simpler task.

You can add to the flexibility—and the complexity—of such an awning by splitting it into two or more sections.

Bamboo Curtains

Wide bamboo curtains will also furnish adjustable overhead sun awning when used on a metal or wood frame, which has sufficient pitch to utilize the force of gravity to roll the curtains down. The curtains are easily rolled up with the draw-cords that are furnished with them. Bamboo blinds do not last more than a few

Sunshade over this terrace consists of lath panels that slide to any position on the welded steel frames connected to roof fascia and low wall at the right. Notice the attractive shadow patterns cast by the closely-spaced lath onto the white concrete below.
Design: Eric Armstrong
Photo: William Aplin

Movable canvas casts solid shade, can be moved about as desired. Each of the four panels slides on rings on three wires. Holes at low points permit rain to drain through; without them, weight of water would soon cause collapse of the entire structure.
Design: The Kenneth Grahams
Photo: Max Tatch

seasons outdoors, but their lifespan can be lengthened by dressing the cords that hold them together with shellac.

In some localities, there are many days when a porch roofed with wire glass makes outdoor living comfortable: It provides shelter from rain or fog, yet admits solar heat that warms the area. When the sun comes out full force, such a porch often becomes uncomfortably warm.

One Northwest family has solved this problem by installing split-bamboo curtains under the wire glass that pull up to cut off most of the sun when it's hot, and are rolled down to let the sun shine in when it is cold.

Adjustable Overheads

Other truly adjustable overheads are generally either an entire roof that adjusts or a roof surface whose parts adjust to admit varying amounts of light or sun.

A good example of the former is a cantilevered roof flap that adjusts from horizontal to almost vertical position by means of an ordinary screw-type auto jack, thus providing shade and protection from wind as needed.

Another effective controllable overhead is a six-foot overhang, the outward three feet of which is a series of open rectangles. Hinged reed shade panels are tucked back under the three feet of permanent overhang in winter so the patio can receive maximum sun. In summer, when maximum shade is desired, they swing out and fasten to outer edge of the open rectangular section.

One patented adjustable roof is made of metal louvers which adjust like a venetian blind to control the sun's rays.

Another shelter which uses movable parts to control bright sunlight but costs less than a metal louver roof can be made of two panels of spaced laths or slats, placed one over the other. The top panel is nailed to the shelter joists. The other slides in a track below. By moving the sliding panel back and forth a few inches, you admit more or less sunlight as you choose. This roof is not weathertight, but in the closed position it is a very effective wind baffle. Even when closed, however, it does not shut off air circulation.

For complete information on how to construct patio overheads of many different kinds, see the *Sunset* Book, *Patio Roofs*.

Here is a wonderfully fresh and pleasing idea. Tent of redwood snow fencing, hung like fabric, rises 18 feet on 2-inch (inside diameter) pipe posts, with pipe braces at ends. The amount of shade it casts varies with the roof angle.

Design: Royston, Hanamoto and Mayes
Photo: Ken Molino

This large sliding canvas awning provides shade in varying degrees for terrace, patio and living area inside. Awning is broken up into four sections, to permit flexible control of sun and shade. A system of pulleys and cords controls position of awning. Each panel is suspended on wires by a series of wood slats so canvas folds evenly against side of house.

Design: J. R. Davidson
Photo: Julius Shulman

Living room windows and semi-circular terrace get sun or shade when and where owners desire it from awning in foreground and its "twin" in right center of photograph. Corrugated metal awnings ride on rollers and tracks at roof fascia and edge of the terrace.

Design: Arthur T. Brown
Photo: Frank L. Gaynor

RIGHT

Awnings may be rolled back to flood the terrace and living room with sun as shown in the photo above—or pulled together to shade desired part of terrace or living room glass.

Photo: Frank L. Gaynor

Ways to Baffle the Wind

Without some protection against it, wind is likely to be a persistent nuisance in your patio.

Near the seacoast, the evening rush of air from the land to the water is likely to sweep through the patio just at suppertime; or occasionally, it might be the reverse, when a damp and chilly wind rolls in, seeking the warmer land. In the dry inland valleys, it may be a parching wind that searches you out on an unguarded terrace.

There are several proven ways of shielding an outdoor room from wind. Basically, all of them act in one (or both) of two ways: they either divert the wind, turning it aside so it misses the protected area, or they baffle it, forcing it to pass through a screen that breaks it up.

Windbreaks of trees, hedges, and fencing both divert and baffle the wind. Part of the wind is forced to go over or around the windbreak, some of it passes through, but meekly. Trees and hedges make excellent wind protectors — but they require several years before their services are felt. Fences provide immediate protection.

Studies conducted by *Sunset* Magazine of the effects of fence structure on wind action have shown, surprisingly, that a slat fence gives the best protection. Wind will roll right over a solid fence, but when it reaches a slat fence, part goes through, part rolls over the top. The two airstreams meet, producing a turbulence that causes the wind to travel farther before it can roll down into the garden. (A report on wind tunnel tests of fences is contained in the *Sunset* Book on fences.)

Glass windscreens are effective, if properly built. They provide protection and view at the same time.

An overhead will protect the patio, of course; some types better than others. A solid, substantial roof is not essential; for light laths, spaced close together, can do an efficient job. An overhead wind baffle requires some careful designing, however, if it is to work properly. For instance, if it is built at too flat an angle, it might act as an airfoil, and try to take off like an airplane. As a matter of fact, it is this critical angle that causes flat roofs to lose tar paper and gravel in a wind storm.

When wind meets a large obstacle, such as the wall of a house, it is likely to act in freakish ways. Turning the back of your house

Sun deck at the foot of a steep hill was long plagued with downhill winds. After experimentation, owner hit on idea of beam-supported lath deflector-shelter combination. Lath or lattice is the most effective windscreen. It breaks wind up into small components, creates turbulence which acts as a buffer to keep wind out of the immediate area. Redwood 1-by-2's were used to build lath surface here.

Design: Dan Saxon Palmer
Photo: Jerry A. Anson

A wall of glass is the logical solution where wind shelter is needed but view or sun's light or heat are needed. Wind sweeping uphill made air around this swimming pool cold much of the year until glass panel wall was installed. Chairs along wall take maximum advantage of shelter, provide a warm spot for swimmers on cool days.
Photo: Ron Partridge

90

against the prevailing wind is no guarantee of wind protection, for the wind may roll right over your house and pour into your patio. One way of preventing this is to build a baffle along the eaves to kick the wind upward, breaking its downward roll.

Sometimes the wind will blow against the face of a building and roll down into the yard, rendering plant and human life miserable. Again, a baffle arrangement will often cure this. A shelter with a concave roof, shaped like a fireplace smokeshelf, will roll the wind back on itself and keep it out of the garden room.

No pat solution or formula capable of universal or nearly universal application to individual wind problems has been found. Factors which affect the flow of air along the earth's surface are so variable and unpredictable that your copy of a neighbor's completely successful baffle or deflector may be a dismal failure.

One fact about wind control—established by experience and experiments—is that it is not necessary to roof an area over completely to control the wind. Start with that fact, study the wind in your own outdoor area, experiment—and you will almost certainly wind up with a satisfactory wind shelter.

Cotton balls on string show wind flow in walled enclosure with interior overhang. Note direction in top series of cotton balls, lesser force of wind against intermediate balls and lack of movement in the lower series. Air movement here does not follow the pattern traced by wind pressure against cones in model below. Overhang on downwind side prevents back sweep of wind.

Photo: John Robinson

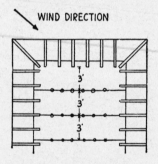

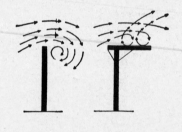

Above, top view of wind shelter pictured at right shows spacing of strings across the room. Side view, below, shows the vertical pattern and spacing of cotton balls.

Diagrammatic comparison of wind flow in enclosure and fenced model pictured on the next page. Overhang, below, counteracts downward movement of air with secondary turbulence, straightens wind flow.

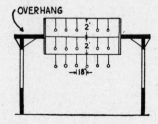

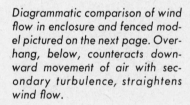

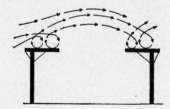

Air movement in this model of a fenced-in yard is traced by paper cones on pegs. Circling air blows lower cones toward fence. Experimentation with various angled fences and different fence positions will show relative positioning necessary for best protection. Topography, buildings around you, vegetation, street patterns and other factors control the wind's effect on your patio.

Photo: John Robinson

WAYS TO
BAFFLE THE WIND

RIGHT

Two efficient wind screens, either of which can be used to provide spot shelter from wind. These panels, of bamboo, and canvas on a pipe frame, work well singly or in series (where a long area is to be shielded from the wind). The steel frame and canvas screen can be moved about with the seasons to block winds no matter what their direction. Sharpened pipe feet drive into the earth easily.

Left photo: Mason Weymouth
Right photo: Theodore Osmundson

Where you have an excellent view, it is only natural to have misgivings about putting up a fence even though the wind may be a real source of disturbance. The hinged screen shown here is a happy solution. It can be pulled out as far as necessary to block the wind, or folded back so it doesn't interfere with the view. When not in use, it folds back against permanent fence in background. Panels of this screen are plywood, but they could just as well be canvas, hardboard, plastic, or burlap.

Design: Lloyd Bond
Photo: Roy Krell

RIGHT

How to block the wind yet retain the fine sea view was the problem in this California beach house patio. Glass wall provided successful solution. Wide overhang and overhead grids help to control winds. Canvas can be lashed over the grids to provide shelter from sun and wind during summer. This patio sunpocket has southern exposure, is usable the year around.

Design: William F. Hempel
Photo: Ernest Braun

WAYS TO
BAFFLE THE WIND

Garage door on extended track has a double life: It ordinarily closes the garage; but, when added shelter from wind is needed in the patio, door slides out to take over the role of patio wind shield. Patio, which is enclosed on three sides, is a four-walled sun room for lounging and entertaining when garage door is opened. Louvered obscure glass panels in the door transmit light and solar heat but assure privacy in the patio.

Photos: John Robinson

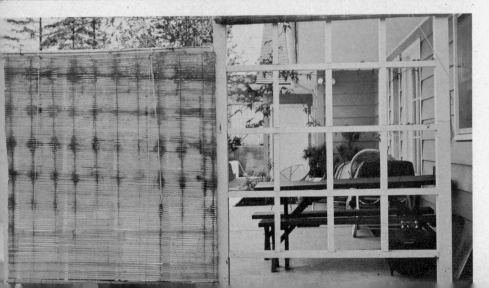

Bamboo shades roll down on side of the screen which catches the prevailing wind. During most of the day, shades are rolled up to reveal handsome trellis-like structure; only toward evening do shades go down to baffle wind and screen out low sun. Bamboo roll blinds last longer if taken down and stored during the winter months.

Design: Chandler D. Fairbank
Photo: Roy Krell

Glass wind screen breaks the wind, mirrors color of the generous-sized planting bed in front, and lets you look through to the green plants and the view beyond. Glass can make an excellent choice for a formal area such as this, but is less adaptable to patios where children abound or where breakage is likely.

Design: Ruth Patricia Shellhorn
Photo: Ernest Braun

This house was built with its back to the wind to protect the small, U-shaped patio. Wind boiled over the house and funneled through the patio at a furious pace, despite orientation. Baffles were installed to deflect wind up and over area—and function to perfection. Wind conditions are so variable that no rules for wind protection can be specific. Experiment to find the best solution.

Photo: Mason Weymouth

Ways to Cool a Patio

In many localities, the sun's rays come beating down relentlessly during much of the patio season.

Different surface materials absorb varying amounts of this heat. For example, a just-watered lawn absorbs only 5 per cent of it; fully 50 per cent of the heat which strikes it is carried off by evaporative cooling. Bare, dry soil, on the other hand, absorbs about 30 per cent of the heat which reaches it.

When you stand under the open sun in an unprotected patio, you are surrounded by a blanket of warm air. In addition, body heat is increased by direct and indirect rays of the sun and heat is re-radiated to you from the earth.

Shade

The simplest and most obvious way to cut off some of the heat is to block the rays of the sun—to create shade. If your patio is not already in, locate it in the shade of the house, on the north side, if possible.

Trees are probably the best all-around answer to shade requirements. Deciduous shade trees provide cool shade in the summer, but let the sun through bare branches in winter. For immediate shade, or as a supplement to tree shade, you will probably need shelter — porches, awnings, lean-to's, freestanding shelters, screens, anything that will keep the sun off the patio living area.

Ventilation

Free circulation of air is your second defense against summer heat. If you are lucky enough to have a prevailing summer breeze, you should do everything possible to keep its movement through the patio unimpeded. Put the patio in its path if you can. If the patio is in, arrange trees, fences, plantings and shelters to provide a path for its passage. Where there is no such breeze, freely circulating air is doubly important to keep the patio from being a heat trap.

Use louver fences, walls and screens. Keep shelter structures as porous and well ventilated as you can with materials like miniature-louver metal screen, lath, or slat roofs, burlap or basket-weave canvas-strip awnings.

Falling sheet of water, made possible by a small circulating pump in this pool, is another accelerator of cooling in any patio. Same principle can be achieved by dropping water over a wood or stone wall, or sprinkling any large surface like the patio floor throughout the hot part of the day. The mere impression of moving, falling water is one of coolness.

Design: H. Van Siegman
Photo: John Robinson

Fountain for this pool is a wide-slotted bake pan, painted with yellow water-proof paint. Rectangular concrete pool is 4-by-3 feet. Inside of pool has two coats of water-proofing paint with color added to match that of the brick. All joints above the water-line are raked clean. Soap flakes give cohesion to water, bluing adds color. Copper tubing connects fountain and pump, pool and pump.

Photo: John Robinson

Reflection

Reflected heat and sunlight can be a planned aid in heat defense. Unplanned or uncontrolled reflection on the other hand, can be an annoyance. A pool spotted in front of an open patio shelter in midwinter can turn on its builder in midsummer by reflecting a blinding glare into the structure. A porch roof of reflective material can deflect vast amounts of glare and heat into an unguarded upstairs window.

Use reflective surfaces — screens, roofs, fences, pools — to bounce sunlight away from your patio. Aluminum in the form of flat or galvanized sheets, shingles, louvers, or heavy foil is an excellent reflector. Galvanized iron reflects well but conducts and re-radiates more heat than aluminum. Substitution of bone-white crushed dolomite for gravel on a tar-and-gravel roof makes it a good reflecting surface. Reflecting pools throw back some of the sun's rays.

Evaporative Cooling

Evaporative cooling is really helpful in defending against summer heat. More than 50 per cent of the heat energy of the sun is used up in the process of evaporation.

Normally, the penalty of evaporative cooling is that release of water vapor into the air increases the humidity and thus off-sets the cooling value of evaporation. In most western areas where summers are hot, however, the air is so dry that the additional water is not noticeable.

Water should be used freely everywhere possible in and around patios in hot, dry areas.

Burlap or canvas awnings or shelter roofs equipped with mist sprayers or other water supply have a marked cooling effect.

The age-old trick of letting water run, drip, or spray over stone walls adds to comfort. Mist sprays or sprinklers achieve more evaporation than a still, wet surface. Sprays in trees and shrubs make evaporative surfaces of leaves, branches and the floor below—in addition to evaporating water directly into the air.

You can make the patio floor an efficient cool panel by mounting sprays in the floor or using lawn sprinklers on it.

Pools are, of course, the basic patio evaporative cooler. Installation of a circulating pump will allow you to increase a pool's effectiveness with a fountain that drops a sheet of water into it, sprays or sprinkles it. (See next chapter.)

Combination of tree shade, ventilated lattice screen and the type of evaporative sprays used in grocery store vegetable departments keeps this patio corner cool on hottest days. Fine mist evaporates faster than still or running water, accelerates cooling. Planning to team cooling devices in a relatively small area results in maximum effect here.

Photo: Jerry Anson

In some localities, every trace of cooling air is welcome during the patio months. Even warm air on the move can help to cool a person. With skillful designing, summer winds can be trapped and channeled into the patio. In this hot-weather haven, the wind is attracted by the louvered fence, slanted to catch it. Open, screened wall also admits fresh air. Sun is excluded by the baffle fence, by the ceiling, and the roll-down bamboo shades.

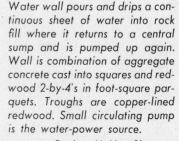

Water wall pours and drips a continuous sheet of water into rock fill where it returns to a central sump and is pumped up again. Wall is combination of aggregate concrete cast into squares and redwood 2-by-4's in foot-square parquets. Troughs are copper-lined redwood. Small circulating pump is the water-power source.

Design: H. Van Siegman
Photo: W. L. Strietmann

A sill was cast around this patio slab so it can be converted to a wading pool for young patio dwellers on hot days. Water cools the concrete, makes it a relatively cool panel when drained for outdoor dining later. Shadow line across this pool is from a pipe which supports a canvas overhead shelter which can be quickly erected to create shade in barbecue area.

Photo: Charles R. Pearson

The sight and sound of water in motion is introduced into contemporary garden with dramatic rain effect in this brick-walled pool. Twelve inches deep, it follows the curved line of a brick wall which terminates in copper slab fountain. Water line is flush with level of patio. Fountain made of 20-gauge copper with soldered joints. Holes 1/32 inch in diameter perforate bottom. Return-pump in pool-wall foundation.

Photo: John Robinson

Patio Pools

There is much to be said for the patio pool. It can serve a number of useful purposes, and the sight and sound of water, introduced harmoniously into contemporary patios, is a pleasingly relaxed element in informal outdoor living.

Pools have undergone a rather complete metamorphosis in the last couple of decades. Pools of all sorts are today related more closely to patio and garden. Water, masonry textures and colors, and plantings are carefully integrated, and pools function easily and unobtrusively.

Swimming and Dunking Pools

Ideally, swimming and dunking pools tie in as additional and very desirable elements in the patio living complex.

A well planned pool is usually convenient to both house and outdoor living area. It is certain to be a major patio landscaping element. Trees and plantings, plus careful orientation with house and patio, can help keep a swimming or dunking pool in its place as a landscaping element.

A full-size swimming pool is a big construction job and a major investment, but it can be a welcome and worthwhile addition to the home—particularly in hot, dry areas without nearby streams and lakes. Swimming pools can be built in a wide range of shapes and sizes for about what you would pay for a new car. For further information, including many pointers for do-it-yourself pool builders, see the *Sunset* Book, *Swimming Pools*.

Planting and Reflecting Pools

Planting and reflecting pools differ mainly in orientation and use. A good reflecting pool must be situated to give easy views of reflected tree limbs and sky, out of the wind so its surface is quiet. Planting pools introduce water and aquatic plant materials into the patio with quiet charm. By careful planning and planting, you can often combine both reflecting and planting functions in a single pool.

A pool can seem hopelessly out of place unless it harmonizes with the design and spirit of the patio of which it is a part. In a garden and patio laid out along simple lines, you would expect

The pool may be small, but the outdoor livability it affords can be limitless. This pool, in Honolulu, is augmented by generous-sized entertaining area made possible by overhead which extends from the house to within a few feet of the pool. In shade, non-bathers can barbecue, dine, loaf. Far side of the pool is for sunbathers.
Photo: R. Wenkam

Living room looks out on a red brick terrace and a large splashing pool for the children. Pool is shallow, but small children have a fine time splashing in it (and parents have less cause for worry). There is an interesting sidelight to the terrace: the bricks were set in sand to allow air and moisture to reach the roots of an enormous old white oak tree, part of which is visible at top left.
Design: Lawrence Halprin
Photo: Ernest Braun

to find a pool that is correspondingly straightforward in design. But when, as has happened with some of the pools shown here, the surroundings and topography point the way to a pool set among rocks or hidden away in a quiet spot sheltered by lush planting, the wise patio builder will follow that lead.

In many cases plants can be effectively used around a pool to create additional interest. They can even be carried right to the water's edge. However, for the most part, pool outlines should be kept clear and uncluttered.

Circulating Pools

Unless you are lucky enough to have a stream or active spring on your property, the circulating pump offers the best way to add the sound and sight of running water to your patio. On a hillside, you can build a waterfall with the help of such a pump. In a level patio, a circulating pump can be used for rain or running water effects (as illustrated on pages 99 and 103).

Brick veneer and white-sand concrete coping of this large pool relate it to white-trimmed brick house, brick patio. Pool water supply and drainage are integral, with controls concealed against house and brick wall. Inset planting rectangles are filled with bog plantings. Plant area at left is occupied with Japanese iris. Water lilies are planted in wood boxes.
Design: Eckbo, Royston & Williams
Photo: Kurt E. Ostwald

"Natural" pool features boulders, smaller rocks, and planting to tie it in with landscape. Water is 4 feet deep by terrace so the children can swim in the summer. Recirculation through filter keeps water clear. At night, light through glass walls of house is reflected in water; also, the entire area can be floodlighted at night.
Design: Michael Wills
Photo: Darrow M. Watt

Concrete, trapezoid-shape lily pool is 6-by-10-feet with a surround of brushed concrete 10-by-16-feet. Pool is two feet deep to accommodate lilies. Lily roots are in pine boxes 18-inches square by 1-foot deep. Use of boxes of fir or pine simplifies operation of dividing bulbs, done every two or three years. You can grow lilies in a pool like this only 8 inches deep if deeper sections are built to hold plant boxes.

Design: Floyd Cowan

PATIO POOLS

LEFT

A small, 12-by-24-foot pool fits into the area between this tract house and the front setback line. A former car port, partially visible qt left, was converted into a pleasant lanai. Decorative fence provides privacy and safety.

Design: Paul Collins
Photo: Ernest Braun

RIGHT

House built around pool brings water into intimate contact with home and garden with striking effect. Pool also helps keep house and deck cool on hot days by evaporation. Concrete pool swings wide around two sides of house, is 4 feet deep at center. Projecting boulders and steel-reinforced stone pier support for deck give natural feeling. Plantings surrounding pool are materials associated with cool, shaded gardens.

Design: C. Jacques Hahn
Photo: Hal Barnes

RIGHT

Concrete-lined fish and lily pool is edged with brick. Following basic principles of Japanese gardening, owners collected rocks and tried them in many different spots before placing them permanently. Korean grass (Zoysia tenuifolia) surrounds pool, with Mondo grass partially surrounding rocks such as traditional Japanese "pedestal stone" in left foreground.

Design: Mr. and Mrs. John Jenkins
Photo: Alex Williams

LEFT

Rock-rimmed pool fits naturally into rocky hillside yard. The large boulders were brought in from nearby mountains. Rough-finished concrete in pool was applied by hand, has two coats of waterproof paint colored to match rock. Despite rough, natural appearance, pool's construction followed standard rules. Plantings of daisies, low rock plants integrate pool with rest of yard. Overflow drainage lets water run down steps to lawn below.

Design: John Dolman
Photo: William Aplin

Ways to Heat the Patio

Truth is that many patios are too cold to enjoy during part of the year in almost any part of the Pacific West. After sundown, just when you want to relax with your guests, a chilling wind is likely to appear and drive everyone to their wraps, or force you to retreat reluctantly indoors. Or, sunny spring and fall days may be just a little too cool for comfort.

Most people will tolerate an air temperature drop of a few degrees without discomfort, but when the thermometer skids below the upper 50's, sweaters and coats are suddenly needed. To a certain extent you can control the temperature of your patio. If the drop is not too severe, you can extend the hours of enjoyment by installing some form of heating. No heat source now economically practicable will warm an exposed patio thoroughly—but you can gain psychological and some physical warmth from radiant heat, fireplace, firepit, or a brazier of glowing coals.

Radiant Heat

Probably the most satisfactory and certainly the most expensive way to warm your patio is with a radiant-heated panel—usually in the patio floor. Such a system, fueled by hot water or electric coils, won't keep you warm on cold, windy nights. But on many marginal evenings when you need only to kick the temperature up a few degrees for comfortable dining or entertaining, it can be a lifesaver.

The radiant panel won't provide the "throw another log on the fire" kind of extemporaneous heat. It is slow to react because of the great mass of reflecting surface which must be heated, so you have to allow two or three hours before its effects are noticeable. Yet, despite these limitations, the radiant panel is the only really satisfactory source of large-area *general* outdoor heat.

To see how radiant heat works, turn to page 115.

Fireplaces

An outdoor fireplace will provide a cheery form of heat to those sitting close to it. The heat of fire in an outdoor hearth travels in straight lines; that is why you feel its warmth in front but not in back when you face the flames. The fire does not warm the air around you—the heated air simply goes up in smoke.

Armed with knowledge about the straight-line habits of fireplace heat, you can take advantage of this peculiarity. Reflecting screens, plantings or walls will bounce heat back and give you

Five-foot-wide firepit provides a friendly, informal gathering place. Circle contains 39 Roman bricks set in mortar. Hole was dug 20 inches deep, filled with crushed rock and top layer of pea gravel. Guests can barbecue over bed of coals, using long-handled forks, skewers, hinged wire toaster.
Design: Arnold Dutton
Photo: Douglas M. Simmonds

Portable "fireplace" made from boiler-head throws surprising amount of heat from a small fire, looks attractive on patio. Boiler heads can sometimes be found in junk yards, but the easiest way to duplicate this project is to take a manufactured metal bowl (available through large nurseries in many cities) and have a metal shop take it from there. Or you can wrap a piece of aluminum around one side of the bowl as a reflector. Movability could be increased by adding casters to legs.
Design: Donald W. Vought, Jr.
Photo: Darrow M. Watt

more warmth than a fireplace that is free to warm all outdoors.

Outdoor fireplaces have their own structural requirements. Because many of them double as trash incinerators, for burning leaves and cuttings for instance, they require more generous flue openings than their indoor relatives in order to carry off the greater volume of smoke. The height of the chimney in many outdoor fireplaces is inadequate to draw off smoke unless it is so high that it looks entirely out of place in the patio. The short chimney favored for outdoor fireplaces because of its artistic proportions is likely to be an inefficient flue. Since you will probably have to compromise on height, your principal requirement is to chop the chimney off at a height that will at least keep the smoke and sparks from billowing back on your guests. Also, don't locate it where the heat and combustion gases will rise into a tree and damage it.

If an outdoor fireplace is to be built within a city, it will be subject to local fire ordinances. Spark screens and other accessories may be required, so check with your building inspector if you plan to install one.

Outdoor fireplaces are fully discussed in the *Sunset* Book, *How to Plan and Build Your Fireplace.*

Cheerful log-burning fireplace adds to usable hours of this Washington State outdoor living-dining area. Native stone masonry blends with house surroundings. Fireplace is lined with heat-resistant brick. It is used often to supplement the sun's heat on still days, providing sufficient boost in temperature to make the area comfortable.

Photo: Chas. R. Pearson

Firepit

The firepit brings the campfire's friendliness into your patio. With a few simple accessories, it can also be used for an effective barbecue.

Easiest provision for a firepit is simply to leave an opening in your patio paving and build the fire on mother earth. A concrete slab will not stand up under an open fire—the heat returns the concrete to its elements: sand and cement. If you want to build a fire *on* the slab, place a protective layer of firebricks over the fire area.

City building inspectors are even more critical of open firepits than they are of outdoor fireplaces, so be sure to check local regulations before you start construction.

With only a few dozen bricks, you can arrange a little fireplace like this in just a few minutes. Semicircle form protects plants behind fireplace. Bricks can be arranged in innumerable ways, or removed during the day.

Photo: Darrow M. Watt

Braziers

Portable barbecues and braziers, especially those with open or screened sides, are a fairly good source of heat for small areas. They have two advantages: You can move them almost anywhere to give quick heat in a limited area, and they throw very little smoke if charcoal is burned, so they can be used satisfactorily in an otherwise unheated garden shelter.

The brazier, like the fireplace or firepit, benefits greatly as a heat source from addition of some sort of reflecting surface. One type of reflector, pictured here, utilizes an inverted-parasol shape to bounce heat back down on a general area. A convex reflector could be used to direct reflected heat to a more specific area.

You can probably resolve your patio heat problems somewhere between the simple earthen firepit and the radiant heating panel. Think about cost, climate and your living habits outdoors before you choose a patio heat source.

If you are concerned only with wind, or if you don't stay outdoors late in the evening, a simple arrangement of screens and overheads may contribute sufficient warmth to make an actual heat source unnecessary. Their disadvantage is that they tend to enclose the patio so it loses its loose, free feeling, and may become a sort of complex maze.

Patio heating is definitely a "plus," but plan it wisely, with discrimination—don't expect too much of it.

Overhead heat reflector shaped like a down-pointed umbrella bounces heat from small charcoal fire in brazier back over much wider area in this covered patio. Reflector is made of two pieces of stainless steel, bent to form a shallow cone. Outer edges are rolled over a circular pipe support. Surface must be kept polished for maximum effectiveness.

WAYS TO HEAT THE PATIO

Radiant-heated patio area, sheltered from wind by a woven-redwood fence, is comfortable "in shirtsleeves" for several extra hours on a cool night. Overhead shelter improves heat: On this night, the radiant-heated area was "not quite warm enough" in the open, "comfortable" under the live oak tree, and "quite comfortable" under the corrugated aluminum and plastic shelter.

Photo: Barry Evans

Half-inch copper tubing coils for patio radiant heat panel cover 750 square feet. A little over 1,000 lineal feet of tubing were laid over a concrete slab and then covered with bricks, laid on a cushion of sand. Water heater is twice the average home heater size. Water is forced through the pipe by a 1/6-horsepower motor, with a pressure of 8 gallons a minute against a 5-foot head.

Photo: Barry Evans

A fireplace can be used to combat temperature extremes, such as this. Patio is rimmed with high sill so it can be flooded and converted to ice rink in winter. Surface is slicked up with application of hot water just before skaters take over. For summer uses of this year-round patio, see page 102.

Photo: Charles R. Pearson

The Patio Barbecue

Sooner or later, a barbecue of one form or another seems to turn up on every patio. It may be anything from a compact portable, barely large enough for a pair of hamburgers, to a great monolithic installation, capable of feeding a horde.

The presence of grill-and-grate in the patio is easy to account for. More than just a fad, it contributes a friendly rite to outdoor living. Anyone who has loafed away an afternoon with a roast sizzling on a nearby spit, or who has watched his own personal steak being broiled under his nose, is well aware of the pleasure that a barbecue can add to patio living.

Permanent or Portable

The patio planner has an early decision to make when he gets to the barbecue on his check list. Should he buy a portable or install a fixed unit? Each type has its adherents.

A portable unit has many advantages. It does not affect your landscaping, because it can be set anywhere. It can be stored when not in use. It can be shifted around to avoid wind, or sun, or to divert smoke from guests.

Fixed units range from simple installations, inconspicuously blended in with the garden or the house itself, to elaborate free-standing structures upon which focus the entire patio design. Whether large or small, a permanent barbecue can add a charming touch of luxury to any outdoor living area. The important thing to remember is that the "monumental" types require extremely careful planning to keep them from overwhelming patio and garden.

Smoke Ovens

The tantalizing flavor and rich mahogany color of smoke-cooked foods tempt many an outdoor cook to buy or build an outdoor smoke oven of his own.

Several types of portable smoke cookers are available commercially. Their metal exteriors have a clean and shiny appearance, and some models have convenient attachments such as an electric spit.

Of the kinds you can make yourself, possibilities are almost limitless. Here are a few we've seen that work well:

The so-called "traditional" masonry Chinese oven. Has a

A good design used once is often worth using again. The shape of this barbecue-firepit repeats the shape of the terrace. Top screen is for grilling. A second screen, six inches lower, holds charcoal. Bricks in end at right are used for footrest. Built-in benches help to make this an inviting corner of the patio.

Design: Henry Van Siegman
Photo: John Robinson

Scale and design of this handsome two-way spit and grill barbecue give it a long, low look. Spit and grill fit into holes drilled in brick at sides of pit. Motor is hidden in compartment to right which is covered with a piece of steel plate. Draft is regulated simply by turning the loose bricks set in the opening in front.

Design: Earle G. Hedemark
Photo: R. Wenkam

chimney-like oven, from the top of which you can hang great quantities of food. Firepit is offset so that grease drippings can't fall on coals to cause unwanted flames or greasy smoke.

A small fire tunnel encased by 40 loose bricks, topped by a 14 by 24-inch sheet of 3/16-inch steel. At one end of tunnel is a flue tile through which smoke passes to a portable oven (available through hardware stores) from which bottom has been removed. Meat to be smoked rests on racks in oven.

A 30-gallon oil drum on wheels serves as smoke oven; a sheet metal firebox, fabricated by a welding shop, is welded to drum.

Checklist

Whatever variety of barbecue you decide to buy or install, remember these pointers:

1. Buy top quality equipment if you plan to use the barbecue continuously.

2. For a permanent installation, buy your equipment first and build the barbecue around it.

3. Install removable metal equipment in a fixed barbecue so it can be stored during winter months.

4. Try to integrate a permanent barbecue with other elements of the garden plan, e.g., combine with storage, fireplace, garden work center, seat wall, etc.

5. Try out a portable in your garden before installing a fixed unit in order to learn where the winds go in your patio during pre-dinner hours. What might seem to be the best spot on your landscape plan may turn out to be the worst because of blinding late sun, poor smoke dispersal, incorrect draft.

6. Don't overlook utility connections. A water faucet will be handy for cooking or clean-up; an electric outlet for plugging in the spit motor, a radio, or lights; and even a gas cock can serve to start charcoal burning or to pinch-hit when the supply of fuel runs out.

7. Once the unit is in operation, its life expectancy can be increased by not exposing the grill or grate to fire any longer than necessary. Fire gradually destroys iron; ashes in the presence of water eat through metal.

8. Break in a masonry barbecue carefully. Do not build a fire in it for two weeks after completion. Then cure it slowly with a small fire, kept burning for four or five hours. Break it in all over again after a rainy winter if it is exposed to the elements.

Versatility combines with sensible design in this three-way example. It can be used as a regular barbecue (note that the grill is in place), as a firepit (with grill removed), or as a smoke oven (with fire in low fire box and food hung inside chimney at rear). Cost of materials was approximately $100, equally divided between masonry (about 400 common bricks and 100 fire bricks) and metal parts, of which all but the grill were custom made. Flared design makes masonry seem less bulky.
Design: R. C. Horne
Photo: Kenneth Cooperrider

U-shaped barbecue area lets the barbecue chef face his guests. Walls are of burnt adobe. Within the "U" a concrete slab supports a divided fire bed—one side for simmer (top of kettle is visible in photo) and the other for broil. Charcoal and kindling is stored beneath slab. Counter serves as buffet. Old school bell summons stray ones to "come and get it!"
Design: Fred Knipe
Photo: Frank L. Gaynor

THE PATIO BARBECUE

This versatile built-in seat is located in the most-lived-in part of the patio, and is a popular relaxing spot during the day. When it is time for the barbecue chef to go to work, chaise longue-type seat cushions are removed, the hinged top is raised, and suddenly everything takes on a new look (see photo below).

Open barbecue has twin iron grills. The stainless steel seat bottom protects wooden bench top, keeps stains off brick wall, can be left open to reflect warmth into living area. This barbecue uses gas as fuel, but could be adapted for use of charcoal.

Design: William Koskinen
Photos: John Robinson

Firepit-barbecue, brick paving, and garden seat brought together smoothly in one continuous unit. Bricks are firebrick—hard-burned red brick. Grill can be inserted in 3/4-inch pipe at four different levels, with iron bars at same level providing support.

Design: Robert J. Tetlow
Photo: John Robinson

THE PATIO BARBECUE

Is there a barbecue on this patio? Looking from the house, you see a pleasant combination of wall, pool, and planting bed. Terrace seems a perfectly natural continuation of the house, quite in keeping with the wooded surroundings. (For what goes on behind the scene, see photo below.)

Looking back toward the house from other side of "wall" in photo above, see how barbecue grill and serving counter are hidden behind the stone wall. A solution such as this is made-to-order for those who think permanent barbecues are "sore thumbs." (There's a "hidden" advantage here for the barbecue chef: He can face his guests while he works.)

Design: Roger Lee
Photos: Larry Kenney

Barbecue made of concrete blocks stained brown and laid dry. To provide a correct draft, a piece of sheet steel is leaned against fire opening. Heat from fire box percolates through hollow blocks, warms aluminum trays and plates at the side. Adjustable spit has permanent shelf and combination grill.

Photo: Morley Baer

Table-top Barbecues

In recent years, a small revolution in barbecuing has been taking place right under our noses. The table-top barbecue has come into its own as a practical, economical, and appealing means of charcoal cooking.

There are numerous and diversified kinds to choose from: brazier and bucket types made in America, cast iron and ceramic ones imported from Japan and popularly called hibachis. You can take your miniature barbecue anywhere in your car. You can cook with it outdoors or indoors. Place it on the patio table; take it on a boat; use it at the beach.

Because you are using fewer coals in a smaller vessel, it takes but a few minutes for hot coals; thus, you can decide to barbecue at the last minute and still have a fire on time. If your miniature barbecue doesn't have an adjustable grill, the quickest way to reduce heat is to remove some of the glowing coals. Fire control on most hibachis is simply a matter of closing or opening the draft door.

BELOW

Three miniature charcoal cookers serve a barbecue supper on the patio to a dozen people. For the adults, chicken pieces are grilled right on the table, which is set for buffet service. Younger set enjoy a barbecue of their own, roasting frankfurters very safely on a portable brazier. Small table in background holds buns, relish, and mustard for each young guest to dress his own hot dog.

Photo: Clyde Childress

Table-top brazier,
adjustable grill

Cast-iron
hibachi

Small
ceramic
hibachi

Portable barbecue,
adjustable grill

Small
table-top
brazier

ABOVE

Miniature barbecues shown here include American-make braziers as well as Japanese hibachis. Grill sizes vary from about 5 inches diameter on the smallest hibachi to 16 inches on the largest portable brazier shown. Many braziers are designed so the height of the grill may be raised or lowered; most hibachis do not have adjustable grills. Hibachis are generally heavier than braziers, but hold the heat longer. Accessories shown below miniature barbecues are (left to right): Small bamboo skewers used for grilling of tiny kebabs, teriyaki, or other appetizers; sukiyaki pan that has removable handle; metal skewers with wooden handles to grill dinner sized kebabs; heavy gloves, needed when working with any barbecue—especially portable barbecues.

BELOW

Bucket cooker, with its convenient handle, is easy to carry to a picnic. Ceramic hibachis are handsome, but will break if dropped; also, either ceramic or cast iron may crack if water is poured on while hot. Small ceramic types are especially attractive to use for broiling hors d'oeuvres in the house. (Caution: no matter which kind you are using, it is generally best to light the charcoal fire outdoors; when coals are glowing, bring hibachis indoors.) Hinged wire toaster is especially useful for grilling and turning tender fish steaks or fillets—also for hamburgers, other steaks. Use metal chopsticks as you would tongs for moving hot coals. Long handled forks are ideal for toasting frankfurters. Skillet is traditional for making Japanese egg rolls.

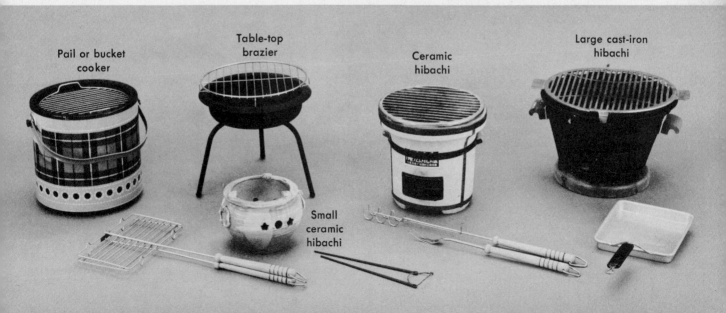

Pail or bucket
cooker

Table-top
brazier

Ceramic
hibachi

Large cast-iron
hibachi

Small
ceramic
hibachi

Garden and Patio Lighting

A well-lighted outdoor living area should do one or both of two things: 1) Invite you out-of-doors at night; 2) bring the beauty of the night garden into view from inside the house. Although there are countless ways to light a garden, all of them fall under one of three general types:

1. *Functional light.* This is for areas that need light, at least at certain times—for example, a pool area, an entryway, a play court (such as for badminton), a parking area.

2. *Esthetic light.* Used for effects—to highlight a shrub or tree, a vine, a fence panel, a piece of garden sculpture.

3. *Combination of functional and esthetic.* A garden path is a good example (you light the way and also the planting along the path). Light shining up into trees illuminates the branches and foliage; at the same time, it reflects back to the patio a light that is soft and subdued, yet bright enough to see by.

For high-intensity illumination, such as might be needed for a patio ping-pong table, bright floodlights or spotlights are most satisfactory. Floodlights are excellent for backlighting of trees. There is a wide choice in styles of lamps—reflectors come in almost every conceivable size and shape. Whatever kinds of fixtures you use, it is best if they are not visible from the house or the patio. Conceal lights at or below ground level, behind plants or masonry, on top of the house or under its eaves. Also, place them so they will not inconvenience the neighbors—a rooftop spot might shine like a locomotive headlight into a nearby bedroom.

If you are putting in a permanent system, check with your electrical inspector to be certain your plan meets local code requirements. You will probably need a permit if you plan to do your own wiring.

You may prefer a portable system that can be set up when needed and dismantled next day. In working with extension cords for temporary lighting, remember that grass is usually wet at night and a shock could be fatal. Use all waterproof cords, outlets, and fixtures. Screw in lamps and plug in extensions when the switch is off.

Do-it-yourself'ers who have qualms about their ability to work safely with electrical equipment may wish to use one of the systems that operate on low voltage. They operate on only 12 volts, and use so little current that there is no danger of shock. A low-voltage system consists of transformer, double wire, and plastic lamps, and is easy to install.

Night lighting with floodlights accents the tree, stepping stones, small pool, and other desirable features of this garden, while the darkness beyond blots out all else —neighbors' rooftops, telephone poles, wires.

Turnabout view of same patio and garden shown in photo above, showing how the house at night becomes a "natural" light source for the patio. Overall effect is to pull the patio-garden area into closer relationship with the house interior, while giving the entire outdoor area an atmosphere of softness and intimacy.

Design: Sim Bruce Richards
Photos: Ernest Braun

GARDEN AND PATIO LIGHTING

LEFT

This fixture, shown in Sunset's patio, was made by lacing a four-foot square of perforated aluminum into a circle and setting it over a photo reflector. Edges are overlapped three holes and laced with wire. Can also be rigged to accommodate an electric light bulb, and hung from tree.

Photo: Blair Stapp

RIGHT

Tropical plants, with their many bold and striking characteristics, are among the finest garden subjects for night lighting. Here, dramatic form of tropicals is accented by a weatherproof metal fluorescent fixture on the ground.

Design: W. Bennett Covert
Photo: William Aplin

LEFT

Japanese lanterns make wonderful party lights. They are inexpensive, colorful, gay, and festive. These paper lanterns are fastened to a string of colored outdoor Christmas lights.

Photo: Clyde Childress

Outdoor Benches

The garden bench of today is a far cry from that of yester-years. The classic stone bench set at the end of a garden path is all but gone. With today's emphasis on outdoor living and entertaining, the garden bench is quite often a part of the patio rather than of the garden—or, perhaps more accurately, it is a tying-together of the two.

Why a garden bench? The most obvious reason, of course, is to provide a place to sit. It may never completely replace other garden furniture, but consider how many extra people can be seated on a 10 to 12-foot bench—on a terrace, by a swimming pool, close to an outdoor game area. There is no need to go rounding up chairs from all over the house and garden, and then have to put them all away later.

Benches come in handy in many other ways. A wide bench can double as a table for summer lunches; a box bench can double as a weatherproof storage bin; a bench that is long enough can be used for sunbathing, covering it with lounge pads for comfort and color.

At times a garden bench may become a garden shelf for the display of plants in containers, such as a bonsai collection or a group of pots of flowering color to be changed with the seasons. Or perhaps you want to show off a piece of driftwood, some interesting rocks, or a stone turtle or fish. If it's a wide bench, there's room for people to sit without being crowded by these displays.

Cushions add a decorative yet practical touch to this handsome low bench. Legs are 4 by 8 by 16-inch concrete blocks. Metal "U" straps are sunk in concrete in the hollow core of the blocks. The top section of the bench is bolted to straps.
Design: Frederick E. Emmons
Photo: William Aplin

Design

A bench can be decorative in its own right. It may be designed as an extension of a wall, fence, or screen. A permanent bench makes an excellent divider and introduces a contrasting element into the garden, in the same way that a raised bed breaks up a flat surface. In fact, one side of a raised bed often forms the principal part of a permanent bench. A related idea puts a retaining wall to work by attaching a bench to it.

Benches with backs have lost much of their popularity in recent years. For one thing, many people feel that a back obstructs the view to the garden beyond. Also, potted plants can be shown off to much greater advantage on a backless bench. However, for those who prefer having something to lean back against, it would be relatively simple to put backs on most of those shown here.

Height. For maximum comfort a bench should be between 15 and 18 inches high, the approximate height of most chairs. Make

Bench around a tree well in the patio is supported by 2¼-inch pipe on outer edges; inner supports are 4 by 4's. Outside measurement is 7 feet square. Young olive tree, being an evergreen, casts shade over some part of the bench at any hour of the day.
Design: Casey Kawamoto
Photo: Darrow M. Watt

it lower if you plan to cover it with a thick mat or cushion. A bench used primarily for sunbathing can be as low as 6 or 8 inches.

Width. There is no set guide; it all depends on how you plan to use the bench. The general range is 18 to 36 inches, with perhaps as much as 48 inches if you plan to use it as a combination bench and table. A bench only a foot or so wide is likely to be both uninviting and uncomfortable.

Checklist

If you plan to build your own bench, here are some pointers:

1. Bench legs should be sturdy enough for solid support and still be in scale with the rest of the bench. To be sure the bench will not sag and warp later on, remember this advice: "Plan the bench to be very sturdy; then build it just a little stronger."

2. Space legs about 3 to 5 feet apart, closer if you use light legs (such as 2 by 4's) or if lumber used for the bench top is narrow and requires more support to prevent sagging.

3. Redwood and cedar are the woods most frequently used for outdoor benches. It is important to use the best grade of lumber for the upper surface of the bench. Lower grades are quite satisfactory for the underbracing and other parts that are not directly exposed to the weather.

4. Use 2-inch-thick lumber on bench tops for strength (1 by 2's or 1 by 3's are satisfactory *if set on edge*). Leave ¼ to ½-inch space between boards, for drainage.

5. To prevent staining of wood, use only galvanized or non-rusting nails, screws, and bolts.

6. To finish or not to finish? It is a matter of choice. Redwood and cedar age gracefully, turning a grayish color in time, and you may prefer not to apply a finish. Or you might wish to put on a water repellent and sealer, which won't alter the natural appearance of the wood (they are colorless) and will tend to eliminate the darkening process as wood weathers. You can apply other finishes over them later if you wish. Penetrating pigmented stains are excellent for finishing benches, and there are many colors and shades to choose from. Most of them leave a flat, no-gloss surface; some may leave a semi-gloss or even a glossy surface, especially if several coats are applied. For a high-gloss surface, use a glossy clear finish; it forms a hard film that is easy to wipe clean. A glossy clear finish can cause sun glare; also, it will probably require more frequent refinishing.

Building an extra-long bench on a gentle curve can give it a graceful, sweeping appearance. This 40-foot-long bench is supported on 2 by 12's with 2 by 4 bracing. Top is made of 2 by 2's. Bench is by a swimming pool.
Design: John Carmack
Photo: Darrow M. Watt

L-shaped bench can be a strong design feature, and lends itself well to informal entertaining because people can face one another while conversing. Bench is supported by concrete blocks.
Design: Eckbo, Royston & Williams
Photo: Aplin-Dudley Studios

OUTDOOR BENCHES

Here's a solid-looking storage bench (5 feet long, 3 feet wide), with tapered sides that help minimize "boxy" look and give sitters some leg room. Bench opens up for storage (see below).

Bench shown in photo above is handy for storing patio gear, such as seat cushions. Notice broom fastened to bottom of seat. Top is weatherproof. Bench could also hold a multitude of children's playthings.

Design: Jack Gibson
Photos: Darrow M. Watt

Post supporting the patio overhead is also part of this 15-foot-long bench. Bracing is hidden from view by a 1 by 4 fascia. Top is of 2 by 6's. Note how bench extends over lawn for several feet, thus helping to tie in the patio with the garden.

Design: Gil Rovianek
Photo: Darrow M. Watt

OUTDOOR BENCHES

This sturdy bench, with metal supports, was made from redwood with a minimum of cutting. Seat was designed long and wide enough to take the standard 24 by 74-inch chaise lounge pad, but pad is not a necessity.

Rear view of bench in photo above. Supports for seat and back were made by a sheet metal fabricator. One 2 by 12 and two 2 by 6's used for seat. Affixed to back are a 2 by 6 (top) and a 1 by 4 (below).
  Design: Robert L. Lamborn, Jr.
  Photos: Robert L. Lamborn, Jr.

Cantilevered bench serves two purposes: As a step-down from the living room to the open terrace; as a permanent terrace bench.
  Design: Burr Richards
  Photo: Dearborn-Massar

Decks for Level Sites

A deck is most logical on a hillside (see pages 54 to 61), but on almost any site it can give a house a feeling of luxury and spaciousness.

Raised above grade and made of a warmer, more "human" material than masonry paving, a wooden deck can be either a transition between house and garden that seems to extend an indoor space outward, or solely a garden element. In either case, it suggests an area clearly for living activities, even though outdoors.

A deck at floor level is particularly advantageous when you are faced with a step down from floor level to garden level, or when your lot has a gradual downward slope in the direction you plan to build your outdoor living area. A deck smoothly extends outdoor living space; it provides a springier surface than concrete or brick; it gives a quick-drying surface. In the case of the sloping lot, a deck can save you many laborious hours of grading and leveling that would be necessary if you were putting in a paved area.

On gentle slopes, a deck may cost more than a paved area of the same size. Whether it is worth it depends largely on the owner's likes and dislikes.

What goes on below?

There are many different kinds of decks and there are various ways of building them. They can be anything from a few square feet of side porch to a thousand feet or more of luxurious outdoor living. They may be supported by massive piers or small concrete blocks, or even cantilevered out over a hillside.

The diagram below, then, cannot be considered typical of all decks. It does, however, show the essential elements of a medium-sized deck on a flat lot. Lumber dimensions and lengths will vary considerably, depending on the deck and how it will be used. Use lumber of good quality.

Area of this deck is more than half that of house. It runs along entire rear wall and beyond. At house wall it is about a foot from ground; at farthest point from house, about three feet. It creates a large area just off family room (rear) and smaller area off master bedroom (foreground). House shades it from afternoon sun. Bench and open fence (far side) are for protection at edge.

Design: Douglas Baylis
Photo: Ernest Braun

The fun of being on this raised deck is something like that of being on an island. Platform provides a generous level area on gentle slope. Its slight rise provides psychological separation from house and from remainder of garden. Its shape brings two trees into one composition, gives a sense of flow to deck space. Concrete-and-pebble walk is a graceful transition to the house.

Design: Douglas Baylis
Photo: Ernest Braun

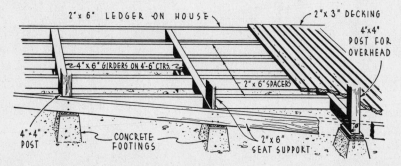

2"x 6" LEDGER ON HOUSE

2"x 3" DECKING

4"x4" POST FOR OVERHEAD

4"x 6" GIRDERS ON 4'-6" CTRS.

2"x 6" SPACERS

4"x 4" POST

CONCRETE FOOTINGS

2"x 6" SEAT SUPPORT

DECKS FOR LEVEL SITES

L-shaped deck across entire rear of house was added as part of a remodel which included substituting a glass wall for the former sparsely-windowed den and enlarging it to family-room size. Result is a new and pleasant relationship between indoors and outdoors. Owners can now live in close proximity to fine old trees on the property.

Design: H. Douglas Byles
Photo: Clyde Childress

A deck such as this can be added to many styles of house (house and lot shown here are part of a subdivision in Sacramento, California). Running nearly the full width of the house, deck is 36 feet wide, covers 320 square feet. Roof is partially covered to provide shade and allow for use of part of deck during rainy weather.

Photo: Morley Baer

Former outdoor living area was a small concrete patio 8 inches below floor level of the house, extending out only a few feet from living-dining area. Raised deck, at same floor level as the house, was simply built over it and on out to fence at rear of the property. Low bench and decorative screening fence tie in attractively and unobtrusively.

Design: Lloyd Bond
Photo: Roy Krell

Deck creates an almost unbeliev-
able sense of spaciousness inside
living room since both floor levels
are even and roof overhang repeats line of the ceiling. Deep roof
overhang gives shade somewhere
on the deck almost any time of day
and helps control west afternoon
sun in the living room.

Design: Lawrence Halprin
Photo: Ernest Braun

Versatility of the deck in an outdoor room is exemplified in this
wind-sheltered interior garden between bedroom and living room.
As a showplace for container
plants, a deck is ideal.

Design: Craig Ellwood
Photo: Marvin Rand

DECKS FOR LEVEL SITES

Attractive deck next to a swimming pool (out of picture) provides additional flat space by bridging over a dry stream bed. Decking is random widths of surfaced, 2-inch-thick, kiln dried redwood. Wood step at end, circular steps at right make it easy to get on deck, which is 16 inches off ground.

Design: Armand R. Ramirez
Photo: Richard Fish

Remodeled house has a generous new deck that bridges the gap between living room and paved surface on one side of the garden. Deck now covers what was formerly an awkward, tri-level patio.

Design: Campbell & Wong
Eckbo, Royston & Williams
Photo: Morley Baer

Small lath-roofed garden pavilion, directly off living room, has a built-in bench, is suitable size for relaxing or for entertaining several guests. It extends out over a small arroyo at the side of the house.

Design: Tryon and Foy
Photo: George de Gennaro

Believe it or not, this deck isn't in the middle of a distant tropical jungle—it's in a canyon near Santa Monica, California. Small deck (10 by 18 feet) is surrounded on all four sides by lush planting. A narrow path leads in to the deck from the left.

Photo: William Aplin

Living Shade...Trees

No man-made sun-trap can equal a tree for sheltering a patio. A tree in full leaf provides shade; it absorbs heat reflected from surrounding surfaces—your neighbor's house for example; and it reduces glare from sidewalks, patio pavement, or the neighbor's windows.

By transpiration, a tree throws off gallons of water into the atmosphere and measurably lowers temperatures. Most important, a deciduous tree is a convertible sunshade. It's a canopy in summer, a scant frame of branches in winter.

Choosing a Shade Tree

You can buy shade trees ready for planting in all sizes and stages of growth. For a few dollars, you can pick up a young tree at the nursery which will begin to cast shade in four or five years. If you don't care to wait that long, you can buy a full-grown tree in a giant box. Buying a large tree in this manner is not as fantastic as it may sound. You would be surprised at how much tree you can get for a cost equivalent to that of building a structural overhead.

Choosing a shade tree will depend on the type of shade you need for your patio.

Globe-shaped or umbrella-like trees cast shade directly below them at noon and give little protection from slanting rays of the late afternoon sun. Certain moderate-sized varieties of ash, elm, and thorn planted in the center of a patio will thus give you the greatest shelter at mid-day, but may not protect you at all in the pre-dinner hours.

Tall, pyramidal-shaped trees, if planted close together in a screen will protect you from the glare of the late sun or from rays bouncing off a lake or the ocean. These trees, of course, provide scant shade when the sun is overhead. Typical of this class are cypress, poplar, eucalyptus, and some of the conifers.

Tall screening trees can branch out in two general ways: their branches may start close to the ground, as do the conifers, or they may fan upwards, like cypress and poplar. Shade trees with low-lying branches cut sunlight away from their bases, affect your plantings; trees with fanning branches allow light to reach ground-level plantings.

In many situations, shade trees need to be grown in combinations: a large, spreading type for direct shade of the patio at mid-

This massive oak was already on the property before construction was started. The owners decided to build their patio around it and now its branches make a high canopy of foliage over their terrace. The paving is of bricks laid in sand so that passage of air and moisture to the roots of the tree will not be obstructed and it will remain healthy.

Photo: Morley Baer

Flowering pear in garden has foliage of a pleasing deep green. In fall the leaves of deciduous types turn brilliant reds and yellows; when bare of leaves in winter, the interesting structure of the tree shows up well. The flowers come on later in the season than those of most spring-flowering fruit trees. It has interesting silvery-grey bark, a good accent for a patio tree.

Design: Floyd Cowan
Photo: John Robinson

day; and a stately line of screen trees to shield it late in the day. Screen planting is also an effective way of protecting the patio from wind.

Spring Flowering Trees

The most spectacular event in any patio garden is the sudden color of a spring flowering tree. And its beauty is all the more appealing because it is so fleeting. To the garden designer the insistence on having this dramatic spring picture is one of the headaches in planning. Some of the flowering fruit trees, for example, may be a delight for one week and an annoyance for the other fifty-one. The designer attempts to settle for the most color without losing year-round benefits.

The objection to flowering trees based on their lack of interest when out of bloom disappears when they are planted in movable containers. A box or tub from 16 to 18 inches square will handle a flowering tree for many years. It's necessary to prune a little heavier than you would a garden tree—and to prune to shape. By limiting root space, the container tends to the dwarf tree.

Your nurseryman can help you choose the best flowering trees for your locality. Usually, you can rely on the flowering varieties of crabapple, cherry, peach, and plum and some varieties of Magnolia.

Garden Fruit Trees

Fruit trees as garden subjects are entirely different items from fruit trees in an orchard. To the landscape architect especially, the fruit of the tree is almost a by-product. He looks at the tree in flower, in leaf, as a structure of bare limbs in winter, as a chore in spraying and pruning, before he considers your taste in fruit. But to the amateur the choice of a fruit tree often is based on his memory of flavors of fruits that may have grown anywhere.

Again your nurseryman will be able to help you, for fruit trees tend to localize themselves. In most Western regions, however, you can grow varieties of apple, apricot, fig, persimmon, plum, peach and quince.

When You Build Around a Tree

A fine tree on your lot is sometimes worth as much as the land itself. Here is ready-made shade, a dominant element to build the patio around.

For mid-day protection, an umbrella-like tree, the Modesto ash, casts a circle of shade. Others good for this purpose are the elm and thorn. In the early morning and pre-dinner hours, this type of tree does not give much protection from the rays of the sun which slant in under its branches. Good for afternoon protection are certain moderate-sized varieties of cypress, poplar and conifers.

Design: Thomas Church
Photo: Philip Fein

The picturesque olive tree in this patio, although it looks as though it had been there from its youth, actually was moved in only one year before the patio was constructed. Note the space left around the tree's base. Boxes and containers hanging on tree make it truly a part of the garden. Without tree, so many bricks might have been overpowering.

Design: Victor Pinckney
Photo: William Aplin

The photographs on these pages show why people like to build their houses and patios around a tree. But they don't tell of the preparation and thought that preceded such a close relationship of house and tree.

Actually there are a lot more than just architectural problems involved. Almost every tree is likely to have a weak limb or two. Most of them are subject to damage by pests. Some are short-lived and may have only a few years of growth left. Some may look healthy and solid, but are dangerously weakened by disease or insects.

Every tree within reach of a house should be examined for serious weaknesses. Dead and diseased limbs should be cut out, cavity work done, and steps taken to eliminate pests and disease. Limbs that hang over the house should be strengthened by cabling them to the main trunk of the tree.

Trouble that can lead to the death of the tree will sometimes arise because of physiological changes which occur, for example, as a result of drastic environmental changes. The tree suddenly may be made part of a well-watered garden. Or it may have its water ration reduced—if the area around it is paved, for instance.

Some very beautiful trees offer annoying problems in the way of pests or diseases. The California sycamore (*Platanus racemosa*), for instance, is subject to red spider in the interior valleys, and to scale in Southern California. Unless these pests are controlled, trees can become defoliated by early summer.

It's wise, almost without exception, to call in a competent tree specialist. He can do all that's necessary to make your tree safe (or advise you to destroy it), and he can help you plan its maintenance.

If an existing tree is located on a hillside, get expert advice before you permit the bulldozers to start work. The soil in which the tree grows must be left intact if the tree is to survive. If soil is cut away from the roots or piled on top of them, the tree is sure to suffer. Low retaining walls will hold soil around a tree that has been left high and dry; a shallow well will protect a tree from soil piled up around it.

When and How to Plant

Safest time to plant a tree is in the fall or winter. For planting techniques, use of trees for landscape decoration and climate control, names and descriptions of many varieties, see the chapter on trees in the *Sunset Western Garden Book*.

Large, lemon-scented gum, its roots contained by concrete sunk below pool level gives delicate shade. This ready-made shade is a good main patio element. The house and garden walls enclose the terrace which is sun-drenched during the day and is wired for radiant heat when the nights grow cold.

Design: W. T. Johnson and
Robert Mosher
Photo: Morley Baer

Living Shade...Vines

Want to subdue the sun, create a pattern on a wall, cover a fence, provide seclusion or shade in your terrace? The right vine can answer any of these problems.

Vines can soften the lines of a severe wall and create an interesting texture. With proper pruning and direction, they can be used to emphasize good structural lines in a patio or to cover up any existing unattractive features that might be too expensive to change.

Vines may be handled in two ways: (1) They may be trained upwards on walls or supports. (2) They may be allowed to cover the top of a structure to produce shade. If trained up the posts supporting an overhang or over the top of an arbor or shelter, they will help to keep the area cool on a hot day. In addition to their shade-producing quality many vines have abundant flowers that bloom in the spring and summer patio months.

Vines have some shortcomings when used in a patio. Many varieties require persistent pruning. Rampant vines can cause a patio to look neglected or to lose its form or individuality. If you train a vine over an eating area, don't be surprised to find leaves and an occasional bug in the soup. Although a vine with sweet-smelling flowers is a great attraction in a patio, you will find that bees may be drawn to it in enthusiastic swarms.

You can plant either annual or perennial vines. If the surface on which you are going to train your vines has to be painted occasionally, a good choice would be an annual vine, such as morning glory or varieties of gourds, as they die down eventually. If you need a quick growing vine to cover up while your permanent vine is getting started, annual vines would be the answer.

For a permanent planting you should consider such perennials as grape, wisteria, or a climbing rose, which are usually slower growing than annuals. If you choose a deciduous variety, you will have shade in the summer, but the sunlight will come through it in winter when you want it. Or you can use an evergreen vine for shade all year round. To provide privacy and interest at different times of the year, it is sometimes practical to plant an evergreen and a deciduous vine in the same area.

For planting suggestions and a list of varieties, see the chapter on vines in the *Sunset Western Garden Book*.

Evergreen grape (Cissus capensis) adds a lush fringe of foliage to roof of terrace; in cold areas use a hardy variety of grape. Grape vines cast interesting shadow patterns and—like most other vines—are superb air conditioners. Leaves give off moisture on hot days, cooling the immediate surrounding atmosphere. Unlike solid covering, a canopy of foliage has open spaces between the leaves that permit air circulation.
Design: Mrs. D. Croftin-Atkins
Mrs. Lockwood de Forest
Photo: William Aplin

Grape vines are classic arbor plants, provide ideal summer shade, fruit (if you plant the right variety), effective winter branch pattern. Notice clusters of grapes in upper left portion of the photo. In an intimate sitting area such as this, there's an esthetic delight in the rustling sound of wind passing through foliage. Grape vines grow rapidly, do their best if given a light annual pruning.
Photo: B. J. Allen

147

Wisteria dangles graceful clusters from an arbor high enough to let you look up into vine. Dark stems are effective against white. Wisteria is obtainable in white, lavender, and pink. Hardy varieties will do well almost anywhere.

Photo: Gladys Diesing

Evergreen clematis (C. armandii) makes a dense foliage canopy. Use silver lace vine or Japanese honeysuckle in cold climates. If you decide on this very popular and attractive variety of clematis, be prepared to carry on a regular spray program—aphids are frequently attracted to it.

Photo: Blair Stapp

ABOVE

Ever notice how cool and inviting a nursery looks when you're out in the sun in hot country? This dining terrace has the oasis-like charm of a nursery. Variegated ivy is trained up trellis supports; sweet pea vines grow on wire across rear wall; oleander hedge in background. Bamboo shades roll down for added sun protection.

Design: H. V. Cowger
Photo: Aplin-Dudley Studios

RIGHT

Variegated ivy makes a foot-thick padding under a roof extension. Slow to get started, it grows rapidly once established. Should be cut back and trimmed annually to prevent bunching, with occasional light trimmings in between times.

Design: Paul T. Wolf
Photo: Richard Dawson

Container Plantings

The artful use of plant materials in a patio often makes the difference between an outdoor room that is passable but dull and one that draws you to it like an oasis on a summer day.

Plantings soften the hard, mechanical lines of fence, bench and wall; they help to cool the patio by evaporation and by preventing glare from the sun's rays. On dull days, they brighten the terrace with their blooms, freshen it with their fragrance. Carefully placed groupings can break up bleak stretches of pavement, lead the eye away from an unfortunate feature of the landscape, or substitute for a missing view.

Plant materials can be introduced into the patio in conventional planting beds, in raised beds that may double as soil retainers or seat walls, or in portable containers that can be placed anywhere on the patio pavement.

Portable Containers

Movable pots, boxes, and tubs are peculiarly suited to use on the patio because they permit you to bring the garden right up onto the pavement. They have a further advantage of allowing you to keep your intimate garden in tip-top condition. New blooms can be brought forward; dying, diseased, and dormant plants can be parked out of sight.

Potted or boxed annuals, perennials, or bulbs can be used as accents of color or design—placed on steps, in a corner, clustered around porch posts or tree trunks. Modular boxes can be effectively grouped in geometric patterns; lined up against the house, along a path, or on the edge of a deck. Like miniature planting beds, these boxes can introduce a mass of color in the patio.

Many large shrubs and small trees grow thriftily in half-barrels or tubs of wood or fired clay. Dramatic foliage varieties can be placed against a wall, where their leaf patterns contribute design interest. Bushy varieties can be used to soften a corner, disguise a meter box, or divert traffic through the patio. Some dwarf fruit trees will produce a blaze of spring color; some will yield edible fruit within arm's reach of the barbecue.

Cultural Tips: Container plants require more water than their garden relatives. Hanging baskets, in particular, dry out rapidly, even when kept in shade. They are more sensitive to extremes of heat and cold.

For planting suggestions and cultural recommendations, see the *Sunset* Book, *Gardening in Containers.*

Many varieties of tulips and sun-tolerant azaleas coincide in their blooming period and make excellent patio companions. Here, pastel lily-flowered and Darwin tulips bloom with lavender, mauve, and white Belgian Indica and Macrantha azaleas in a cool corner. Use of pots is successful here because they have been collected in groups large enough to catch attention.

Design: C. Jacques Hahn

Pots of succulents march up steps alongside retaining wall. Succulents are nearly perfect container plants. They are easy to plant, easy to grow, good looking all year, and they live a long time. Occasionally forgetting to water them will not set them back, as is the case with many container subjects. A sandy soil mix and good drainage are the two main essentials.

Photo: William Aplin

CONTAINER PLANTINGS

LEFT

Squat wooden box is in excellent scale with the low brick wall, is stained the same gray color as the furniture. The plant is blue-gray agave, handsomely set off by a mulch of white gravel.

Design: Georg Hoy
Photo: Darrow M. Watt

LEFT

A bonsai display makes a real conversation piece. This display, in Sunset's own patio, includes some fine old classic bonsai imported from Japan, as well as several younger, locally grown examples. In growing bonsai, key requirements are maintaining the proper degree of soil moisture, atmospheric humidity, and protection from hot sun and drying winds.

Photo: Clyde Childress

RIGHT

Terrace of exposed aggregate keeps its orderliness but still gives impression of a regular garden by the use of raised planting spaces. These are not strictly containers, but they do have the container feeling without the disadvantage of restricting roots. This is a good way to grow plant materials that require too much root space for most containers.

Design: Lawrence Halprin
Photo: Philip Fein

Next Step: The Lanai

No visitor returns from the Hawaiian Islands without having added to his vocabulary at least one new term in architecture—lanai (lah-NIGH). This is a word that may soon be as widely known as "patio."

You often acquire the word so gradually that, back home, you are hard put for an exact definition. But you recall with enthusiasm its elements: green growth, shade, rain protection, an open circulation of air; a view of garden, seashore, or mountains, near or far; wide comfortable places to sit, or sleep; in short, the spot where you talked, lounged, ate, drank, and spent some of your happiest hours in the Islands.

As a Westerner, you felt very much at home in the lanai. It was an informal room. More than one of its elements seemed familiar. You remembered a barbecue in Monterey, a garden house in Pasadena, a wide porch in the Sacramento Valley, a recreation room in Seattle.

If you doubt the kinship of Western and Hawaiian lanais consider this official description worked out by the Honolulu Academy of Arts for an exhibition on "The Lanai": ". . . glassed or walled in on the side of the prevailing winds, and screened against the invasions of moths and mosquitoes . . . the lanai, or outdoor living room planned for special living purposes and incorporated into the basic design of the house . . . has now, in Hawaii, become the most used living area in most homes and serves as a transition between house and garden."

When you talk in those terms, you could be on our West Coast. More than one Westerner has developed a lanai which the Hawaiian would accept without moving a fern or a piece of furniture. It is pure accident of language, the lack of a word that truly captures its spirits, that the Western lanai has been given so many other labels—porch, garden room, tropical room, barbecue, shelter. Why not lanai?

A Southwestern lanai might benefit by more evaporative cooling pools, and mist sprays than is advisable in humid Hawaii. A Northwestern lanai might use a skylight roof to step up the impact of sun. In both, a fireplace or radiant-heated floor would warm up winter days and cool evenings. And some climates might call for movable panel overhead, a choice of shade or sun.

The well-developed porch, or shelter, or outdoor living room next to the house, is the Western lanai. It can extend kitchen or bedroom just as well as living or dining rooms. It is the ideal televi-

Open-air room in San Diego has such "indoor" accessories as cushions, fiber rug on the brick floor, paper Japanese fish decoration, picture on the wall, and lighting in cove and garden. Even furniture is of the variety you can use indoors. This kind of transition-zone room, between indoors and outdoors, may need more or less protection, depending on local climate.

Design: John Lloyd Wright
Photo: Ernest Braun

sion room, children's room, overflow room where either children or parents can entertain.

All these are legitimate lanai variations. For lanai is not a fixed form either here or in Hawaii. It is still developing, still adding refinements.

Converting a Patio to a Lanai

Many Westerners start out with an open patio and gradually convert it to a lanai.

First, they roof it over to keep out the direct sun and to hold the lingering afternoon heat into the evening hours. Then they wall in one or two sides to thwart the wind. Finally, they close over the open side with doors, screen, or glass so they can really use their favorite room all year long. What started as an outdoor living room, imperceptibly becomes another room of the house. But it is more than just "another room," for in the process of disappearing indoors, it takes on the relaxed, luminous qualities of the comfortable lanai.

Almost any patio can be converted to a lanai, but it is not a simple task. Unless you are an expert home handyman, it is wise to call in a contractor to do all or most of the work. If you are the kind who likes to have a hand in the project, you'll find many how-to tips in the *Sunset* Book, *Remodeling Your Home*.

TOP RIGHT

A good sun control system is a necessity for any lanai, if it is to achieve maximum livability. This effective solution, in Honolulu, has an overhang which shades the lanai at noon when sun is highest. As sun declines, to right, slats block direct rays. Awning can be rolled down from horizontal projection at right when sun is lowest; above it, louvers are set at 45° angles to block sun but allow air passage.

BOTTOM RIGHT

Same lanai as in photo above, viewed from outside, shows how sun control is built into three sides. Horizontal louvers (right) shade a breakfast area from morning sun. Vertical slats (center) cut daytime glare. Projecting member (left) holds roll-down awning for late afternoon sun.

Design: Bradley and Wong
Photos: R. Wenkam

LEFT

By simply screening their ranch house type of front porch, owners gained a small, bower-like lanai. Now the porch provides enough opening on the leeward side to draw the prevailing westerly breeze through the house—without insects. Screening also provides some privacy without interrupting the outward view.

Design: Marvin T. Bonds
Photo: Joe Munroe